MESSENGER OF LOVE

MESSENGER OF LOVE

Essays

Compiled by
Wildorf E. Goodison-Orr

Exposition Press   *New York*

EXPOSITION PRESS INC.

50 Jericho Turnpike   Jericho, New York 11753

FIRST EDITION

0-682-47377-4

Dedicated to the truth of the Jesus Christ potential in man and the reality of the omnipresence of the Christ. Through love and the act of loving, the reality of this potential and presence becomes a constant experience.

ACKNOWLEDGMENTS

Very grateful thanks are expressed to the following publishers, copyright holders, and authors for permission to reprint excerpts from their works.

Doubleday & Company, Inc., New York. "The Prayer That Is Love" and "When We Love" from *Prayer the Master Key*, by James Dillet Freeman, copyright 1968 by James Dillet Freeman. "To Justify the Injustices" and "The Work of Love and Intelligence" from *Happiness Can Be a Habit*, by James Dillet Freeman, copyright 1968 by James Dillet Freeman. "When We Look With Eyes of Love" and "People Are Like Poems" from *Look With Eyes of Love*, by James Dillet Freeman, copyright 1969 by James Dillet Freeman. "Why Not Be Nice . . ." from *The Right Answer*, by James A. Decker, copyright 1967 by James A. Decker. "The Power to Be: Love" from *Your Power to Be*, by J. Sig Paulson, copyright 1969 by J. Sig Paulson. "There Is God," "Our Finest Hour" and "The Lesser Good" from *Seed of the New Age*, by Sue Sikking, copyright 1970 by Sue Sikking.

The above reprinted by permission of Doubleday & Company, Inc.

Harper & Row, Publishers, Inc., New York. "From the Mire of Discord To the Miracle of Love" from pp. 156-161, 161-164, 168-169, 171-173 in *Unity of All Life*, by Eric Butterworth, copyright 1969 by Eric Butterworth. "How God Forgives" from pp. 149-153 in *Discover the Power Within You*, by Eric Butterworth, copyright 1968 by Eric Butterworth.

The above reprinted by permission of Harper & Row, Publishers, Inc.

Unity Books, Missouri. "Why Should I Love," by Mary Rowe. (Reprinted from *Unity* magazine.) "Letters of Myrtle Fillmore," by Myrtle Fillmore. "The Grace of God Is Upon You" from *God Never Fails*, by Mary Kupferle. "The Yoke of Yesterdays," by Richard Lynch. (Reprinted from *Unity* magazine.) "Love Fulfills the Law," by Stella Terril Mann. (Reprinted from *New* magazine.) "Love" from *Christian Healing*, by Charles Fillmore. "My God Is Love," by Wildorf E. Goodison-Orr. "The Capacity of Love," by Irwin Ross. (Reprinted from *New* magazine.) "The Priceless Ingredient," by J. Sig Paulson. (Reprinted from *New* magazine.) "Try This Experiment" from *Health, Wealth and Happiness*, by Lowell Fillmore. "Talks On Truth" from *Talks On Truth*, by

Charles Fillmore. "What Is Peace" from *A Letter to Adam*, by Sue Sikking. "The Night the Hippies Prayed," by Alfred I. Tooke. (Reprinted from *Weekly Unity*.) "Sky Prayer," by J. Sig Paulson. (Reprinted from *Weekly Unity*.) "The Love Vibration," by Catherine Ponder. (Reprinted from *Unity* magazine.) "Choose Love Or Perish" by Charles Lelly. (Reprinted from *New* magazine.) "Because He Is Love," by James Dillet Freeman. "The Altar of God," by William L. Fischer. (Reprinted from *Unity* magazine.) *Teach Us to Pray*, by Charles Fillmore. "It Never Dies," by Peggy Sue Sikking. (Reprinted from *Weekly Unity*.) "The Irresistible Power of Divine Love," by May Rowland. (Unity pamphlet.) "Divine Love the Catalyst," by Fred Beale. (Reprinted from *Weekly Unity*.) "Do Not Judge Others" from *The Emerging Self*, by Ernest C. Wilson. "Your Greatest Power" from *Your Greatest Power*, by Elinor McDonald. "Command Performance," by J. Sig Paulson. (Reprinted from *Unity* magazine.) "The Prospering Power of Love," by Catherine Ponder. "What Is Good About Good Friday," by W. E. Goodison-Orr. (Reprinted from *Weekly Unity*.) "God Is My Father," by J. Sig Paulson. (Reprinted from *New* magazine.) "Unity and the Science of Man," by Charles D. Lelly. (Reprinted from *Unity* magazine.) "The Love Commandments," by J. Sig Paulson. (Reprinted from *Unity* magazine.) *Keep a True Lent*, by Charles Fillmore. "The Search for Personal Freedom," by Eric Butterworth. (Reprinted from *Unity* magazine.)

Frederick Landwehr. *The Magic Presence*, copyright 1935 by St. Germain Press. *I Am* discourses, copyright 1940 by St. Germain Press. *Unveiled Mysteries*, copyright 1939 by St. Germain Press.

Ernest C. Wilson. "The Heart of Christ" from *The Contemplation of Christ*, by Ernest C. Wilson, copyright 1970 by Ernest C. Wilson.

Helen Garver. *Brother of the Third Degree*, by Will Garver.

Rabbi Bernard Hooker. "The Bible, Judaism and Jamaica" from *My Brother's Keeper*, by Bernard Hooker, copyright 1969 by Bernard Hooker.

In addition to those whose contributions appear in this book, my heartfelt gratitude goes to Marjorie Goodison-Orr, Berton C. Coffey, V. Stanford Hampson, Bert Cloos, Johnnie Colemon, Florence Anderson, Charles Roth, Denis Robinson, Don Nedd and Sri Chinmoy. And to those who have helped in the preparation of the music and the manuscript—Carol Knox, Linda Stockhausen, Shirley McKenzie, Georgina Soanes and Gloria Graham —this is my expression of LOVE.

—GOODIE

Contents

The Why of This Book

When you are viewing arid land, do you not think that it seems to be interceding for water? Have you observed its response when the blessing of water is poured upon its receptive strata? It absorbs it into its inner self, and then gives to the vegetation which it mothers, and a rich and healthy growth results.

In order that the idea of producing this book could flow through me, there must be a need in me for a greater understanding and expression of LOVE. I hope that I, and the billions of people whom I suspect could be like me, will be led to respond in the way of LOVE.

I know myself to be guided and motivated to work on this idea, by the spirit of UNIVERSAL LOVE, which is individualized in me: and because this omnipotent spirit of LOVE would find expression through all God's children, I expect this production to be received by millions of people all over the world.

From my own observation, I have been inspired to understand many things. I have seen a harmonious family torn apart by allowing ignorance to dominate their spirits. The rift continued for some time, with mother at variance with daughter and father; and father in disagreement with sons and others of the family. It came to an end suddenly when tragedy struck and one of the group experienced a sudden mangled end. Did this *have* to happen to restore the former good relationships which that family enjoyed?

I have seen a married couple living together for years, in a home as silent as a tomb. There was no communication, or goodwill, no LOVE. They worked in the day, and it seemed to me that they both died when they separately entered their portals in the evenings. Then one night tragedy struck, and one was bludgeoned to death by a prowler in the home where LOVE was absent. Loved ones mourn, and the mourners grieve, particularly when death moves in so suddenly. The sad-faced would-be comforters are quick to identify the occurrence with the "Will of God." How utterly false! When there is an absence of LOVE in an individual, in a family, in a world, the gates are left wide open for the entry of every type of ill, tragedy, violence, destruction, and death.

Why did the Master Jesus—who was the *WAY*, the *TRUTH*, and the *LIFE*—emphasize the great need for LOVE? Why did other illumined souls before His Ministry and since, try to get the same message across to mankind? That their efforts have been effective there is no doubt whatever, but in an exploding, restless, hasty, and ofttimes selfish world of people, the expanding vibrations of this harmonizing energy are increasingly essential.

The spectrum of thoughts in this compilation may be viewed as the components of a great big diamond. It is not locked in a vault, nor is it stored under glass with the protection of alarms and other subtle devices. It is a precious gem that you can hold in the "palm of your mind," scrutinize, caress, view from its various facets, see and feel the reality of its rays, assimilate its energy, share its luminance and its pricelessness with others without thought of depletion or loss. It is forever yours, and yet it belongs to the Universe. If you can be perpetually thrilled by the ecstasy and the effulgence of a precious gem, why should you bend backwards to bring into your life and world, a mass of dross, or an infusion of decay? Such an unparalleled gem is the power of LOVE—and the action of LOVING.

This anthology represents the consciousness of many individuals significant of universal unity—which is LOVE. May they wherever they are, be illumined to receive and to give a greater outpouring of Christ Light and LOVE to a world that thirsts for greater peace and harmony.

May those who read these pages thrill to an appreciative understanding of their access to this precious gem, enjoy a renewal of mind, and relish a sustained blessing by the conscious application of its power in their lives.

WILDORF E. GOODISON-ORR (Goodie)

I AM A MESSENGER OF LOVE

W.E. Goodison-Orr
UNITY OF JAMAICA

A Prayer: Let It Be!

Let the Light of LOVE illumine all those who read these pages. Let the illumination of LOVE be a light to all who absorb its messages.

Let health be the manifestation in all who allow the healing, cleansing power of LOVE to flow freely through them.

Let Prosperity, Happiness, and Peace of mind be the only way of life for all who in serenity accept the idea of being loving, and make themselves expressers of the pure Christ LOVE.

As we thrill to the LOVE of our dear ones close to us exuding a fragrance all its own, so is it possible to expand this feeling of goodwill to include all persons everywhere in the acknowledgment of God as Father of us all.

Let the words written herein help to cement and harmonize the people of all races and all countries. Let them be the illuminating influence for all children. Let them touch and inspire the lives of, and be understood, accepted, and applied by adults everywhere in all places, capacities, trades, professions, and vocations. So that the Light will win in enfolding the Universe, peace and good relationships will abound in all people and every person will know himself to be a child of God and a "Messenger of LOVE."

Father God, this is my Prayer. Let it be!

From the Mire of Discord
To the Miracle of Love

On every hand today, at home and abroad, we are facing crises of human conflict: armed forces doing battle with armed forces, hostility across the peace table, militant peace and freedom advocates meeting increasingly militant opposition, the seething unrest in the ghettos owing to problems of social and economic discrimination, and the general struggle between labour and management which often approaches an economy-destroying impasse. One often wonders, "Where will it all end?"

Sometime ago I stood in stunned silence in the American Military Cemetery in Manila, looking out across acres of white crosses. Realizing that each cross represented a soldier who was pressed into service in a war which, in the passing of time, appears to have solved few of the world's problems, I found myself crying out, "Surely there must be a better way."

Again and again we hear the defense of militant action, "We have tried everything else." Have we? Have we really tried the way of LOVE? I am not referring to sentimental or romantic LOVE. Those are but vague and sometimes poor reflections of the dynamic energy of LOVE. It has always concerned me that LOVE is rarely talked about except through the stereotyped clichés of religion, or in the context of the emotions. It seems to me that LOVE may well be the greatest undeveloped resource of mankind. The time must come when mature people will think of LOVE in completely practical terms as a vital alternative to strife, when people in conflict will wisely propose that "what we need now is to approach our differences in the spirit of LOVE."

Professor Sorokin said: "The unforgettable lesson given by the catastrophes of this century convincingly shows that without increased production, accumulation, and circulation of the energy of unselfish LOVE, none of the other means can prevent future suicidal wars. The mysterious forces of history seem to have given man an ultimatum: perish by your own hands or rise to a higher moral level through the grace of creative LOVE."

What is this mysterious energy of LOVE? I am not sure that we have a workable definition, or that we should even attempt to define it. Oh, there are many dogmatic statements about LOVE. No theologian or philosopher is worth his salt unless he makes a clear statement on the subject. Once stated, the matter is settled. However, LOVE cannot be settled or disposed of by definitions, for it is involved in all life. It might be better to unsettle our thoughts about it.

LOVE and life are inseparable from each other. Where there is life, there is LOVE. Even the most primitive form of life is forever trying to burst out of its limitations and experience some kind of unity with other forms. Though each form is separate from other forms, in reality they are all expressions of the same unity of life. There is never any absence of LOVE in the unity of all life. The apparent lack of LOVE is simply the absence of self-knowledge and self-control.

LOVE is the active principle of unity. Everything loves, and everything responds to LOVE. It is a universal quality. It is shared alike by mankind, by the animal kingdom, and by flowers and trees and all growing things. Luther Burbank used to speak to his plants and tell them what he wanted them to do. He believed that there is One Intelligence in everything that responds to intelligence. And apparently it did. Some extensive research is being done with plants, using the polygraph (lie detector device). Carefully controlled experiments prove conclusively that the thoughts and feelings of people have a profound influence upon the growth and vitality of flowers and plants. We now know that the "green thumb" of the gardener is more accurately the "red heart" of his LOVE for the plants and their response to that LOVE.

Larry Trimble, who trained the dog, Strongheart, and one of the world's greatest authorities on dog training, at one time actually slept with a pack of wolves in Canada. They were in captivity but they were untamed. He admits this would not have been safe for most people, but he says he talked to them and told them of his LOVE for animals. They understood him. They weren't afraid of him because they knew he wasn't going to hurt them.

A teacher was being honored because it was discovered that an amazing number of prominent people had come from her little one-room schoolhouse. She said she didn't think she deserved any honours, for she did not have the broad educational background that modern teachers have. She said, "Why, about all I had to give my students was LOVE. . . ." It seems likely that there is a "green thumb" for teachers as well as for gardeners. It has little to do with tuition and technical skill and everything to do with intuition and LOVE.

A doctor, called to a home to look at a seriously ill child, felt an oppressive atmosphere immediately on entering. As he looked at the parents he found anger, suspicion, bitterness, and hatred. He examined the child, who had every evidence of a serious heart and circulatory deficiency. He told the parents that the child would not live six months unless something were done. They said they would do anything. He told them that medicine probably could not help, but perhaps LOVE could. He talked to them about their discord. It seemed that a relative, an in-law, had come between them, creating a bitter problem. The doctor told them to make a decision: did they want these ill-feelings, or did they want their child? They could not have both. He left them to think about it.

One week later, the doctor returned. He immediately sensed a fresh air of LOVE. He examined the child, and there was evidence of a returning to normalcy. The parents thanked him for saving their lives . . . and the life of their child. The mysterious energy of LOVE had worked its miracle.

How often it is glibly said, "What the world needs is LOVE!" I have used the theme myself on several occasions. The statement is correct as far as it goes, but as with so many religious generalizations, it doesn't go far enough. If we tell the couple harassed by marital dispute that all they need is LOVE, they might agree. "Sure, all we need is LOVE, but you see, we don't LOVE each other any more." We have thought of LOVE, like the weather, as something we can do little about. LOVE either happens or it doesn't. We "fall in LOVE" as if by accident. Or we occasionally chance upon a friend whom we can LOVE. But it is a completely unpredictable thing.

Psychology has stressed that the great need of man is to be LOVED, and that many of his problems stem from the absence of LOVE in his life. This, too, is right as far as it goes, but it simply doesn't account for the whole of man. Of course we all need to be LOVED, but how can we solve the problem? Everywhere people are crying out for LOVE. Many of the strange things people do and the games they play are really their subconscious needs crying out, "Won't someone please LOVE me?"

The great need is to be LOVED, but the only way man can be LOVED is by the flow of the cosmic energy of LOVE from within out. No person can give LOVE to another person. All he can do is give expression to the energy of LOVE which creates an atmosphere in which another person's growth process may be reactivated and his LOVE potential released. The great need of man is to LOVE. There is never an absence of LOVE. Problems which we say are caused by a lack of LOVE are really caused by an ignorance of life and the frustration of the LOVE potential in the individual.

The deepest need of man is to express LOVE. Man is a channel for the expression of the transcendent power of LOVE. It is the very nature of the Infinite. The only way the person can be LOVED is from within, as he lets himself be LOVED by the activity of God flowing through him in what Teilhard calls "the attraction which is exercised upon each conscious element by the center of the universe." He says, it is the "call toward the great union, whose attainment is the only real business in Nature. . . ."

Erich Fromm has made some important statements about LOVE. His book, *The Art of Loving,* is a must for the student of the unity of all life. He says: "LOVE is not primarily a relationship to a specific person: it is an attitude, an orientation of character which determines the relatedness of a person to the world as a whole, not toward one 'object' of LOVE. If a person LOVES only one other person and is indifferent to the rest of his fellow men, his

LOVE is not LOVE but . . . an enlarged egotism. Yet, most people believe that LOVE is constituted by the object, not by the faculty. In fact, they even believe that it is a proof of the intensity of their LOVE when they do not LOVE anybody except the 'LOVED' person. Because one does not see that LOVE is an activity, a power of the soul, one believes that all that is necessary to find is the right object—and that everything goes by itself afterward. This attitude can be compared to that of a man who wants to paint but who, instead of learning the art, claims that he has just to wait for the right object, and that he will paint beautifully when he finds it. If I truly LOVE one person I LOVE all persons, I LOVE the world, I LOVE life. If I can say to somebody else, 'I LOVE you' I must be able to say, 'I LOVE in you everybody, I LOVE through you the world, I LOVE in you also myself.'"

LOVE is a universal energy, a divine activity, and not simply the plaything of human volition. Each person has a vast estate in the universe which he hasn't even ventured into. He is like a bird whose experience of life is within the four sides of his small cage. Everything outside the cage is too big for him to comprehend. There is a power of LOVE that is so transcendent to the LOVE we feel for one another, it is beyond comprehension. Still, we long to experience it as the blind man longs for light, because without it we are missing the wholeness of things. More than this, our very longing for it is the intuitive feeling that it is a potency within us seeking releasement.

Why Should I Love?

"Why should I bless those who despitefully use me?"

"Why should I turn the other cheek to let him hit me again?"

"Why should I give him my cloak when he has already stolen my coat?"

"Why do I have to Love my neighbour?"

"Why do I have to Love myself?"

"Why, even for God's sake, do I have to do all these things?"

Let's counter these questions with another:

"Would you like to be enduringly happy?"

We may well ask why Jesus suggested that we do all these things. We may well ask why we should be any happier for resisting the temptation to hit back—to take back what is ours —to curse the person who is mean to us—to ignore the people we simply don't care for, or even heartily dislike.

It's difficult teaching such lessons to others—those who haven't yet experienced the advantage of following Jesus' examples in living. It's not easy to change a whole way of life, unless there is a guarantee that things will be better afterward. Is the only reward of being good, the knowing that you have been good?

Morse discovered that the telegraph would help us to communicate with people quickly.

Long discovered that ether would make us oblivious to sometimes unavoidable pain.

Orville and Wilbur Wright discovered that an airplane could lift us above the earth and transport us quickly.

Judson discovered that a zipper would simplify many difficult fastenings.

Birdseye discovered that frozen food would feed us, when other food was not available.

Whittle discovered that a jet engine could carry us faster than sound.

Roentgen discovered that an X-Ray would enable us to see through seemingly solid flesh.

Hunt discovered that a safety pin would join just about anything.

And Jesus discovered that Love is the fuel that will make the world go round just as it should.

We could be quite dispassionate about this, and call Jesus a super-scientist. Perhaps, after all we have clouded His issues. We have made mystery where there should be none. We have completely lost sight of the fact that Love has been recommended to us, not so we can feel that we are being good, and not so we can say that we are obeying Jesus' instructions. Not so we can confidently attend church, knowing that we are acceptable citizens. Not so we can be sure that we are obeying Biblical commandments. No! We use Love because it is the only fuel that can be used in the smooth movement of the universe.

Only Love can end wars. Only Love can allow us to walk to safety wherever we go. Nothing else can permanently heal. Nothing else can help us to have harmony in our human relations. There is nothing else that will persuade a mother to feed her child. Only Love insures that a husband will work for and protect his family.

Do we have an alternative to Love? Can we say, "Thank you Jesus, and all other teachers who advocate Love, but I know of something better?" Can we say, "I have been happy all my life, and I haven't loved at all?" Can we say "Thanks, but I tried it, and it didn't work?"

One can almost imagine that Jesus thought sometimes: "Will they never get the message? What do they think I am telling them this for? Don't they realise I am telling them how to be happy—and isn't that what they really want? Don't they know this is not just a figment of my imagination, but that this is my contribution to the world? Do they think this is just a mystical, fanciful illusion? Don't they yet see that this is the great discovery?"

Oh, the patience of Jesus! The understanding, the persistence, the unselfishness which He showed the world. How Jesus

Loved! And because He Loved, what a joyous legacy He has left us, what happiness He has bequeathed us, and, in spite of His trials and tribulations, how happy He seemed to be throughout His life!

This is His promise, if we pursue the path of Love: ". . . in the world you have tribulation; but be of good cheer. I (Love) have overcome the world."

We have benefited, all of us, from the discoveries of Morse, Long, the Wrights, Judson, Birdseye, Whittle, Roentgen, and Hunt. Does it seem reasonable for us to turn our back on the discovery of Jesus? Shall we refuse to benefit from Love? Shall we continue to be unhappy, frustrated, unfulfilled, unloved because we are too stubborn to try His way? After all, this gift has been given to us "on a silver platter." We didn't have to work for it. We didn't even have to discover it. We just have to accept it and put it to use. And we have even been shown how to do this.

Why should I Love? Because it's to my advantage. Because I shall be filled with peace and life and success. Because it is the sensible, obvious, and reasonable thing to do. And if I should feel, sometimes, that this universe is precariously close to grinding to a halt, I shall try to remember that the fuel which will get it going again—not just ambling along, but spinning smoothly as it should—is Love. And I shall pour that fuel into every situation that presents itself to my mind, near and far. But perhaps particularly, I shall remember to use it in my day-to-day encounters with people and situations that are all too familiar to me . . . so familiar that I may be tempted to pass them by, not realising that these are points where I must pour in the fuel of Love.

Why should I Love? Why do I want to be happy?

The Master-Craft of Love

Let us consider the quality that is the most refined spiritual attribute that man has. This is the quality of Love. In its spiritual expression, love makes of man a god. But when it is misrepresented, it turns him into a very devil. Love, properly expressed, has been responsible for some of the most beautiful accomplishments in the world. But when it has been improperly expressed, it is responsible for things as unfortunate as murder. In all the teachings of Jesus Christ, none is more direct and far-reaching than what he taught about Love. But, even though he taught it directly and simply, many persons are unable to understand the implications of what he said concerning love.

May we delve into this quality of love, to see if we can get more insight into what it is really all about. In understanding love, we may apply it to benefit ourselves and the lives we touch. Willa Cather, in her book *Shadows on the Rock,* made this rather provocative observation: "Sometimes a neighbor whom we have disliked a lifetime for his arrogance and conceit, lets fall a single commonplace remark that shows us another side, another man, really; a man uncertain, and puzzled, and in the dark like ourselves."

I guess all of us have had the experience of having to deal with, or live with, someone whom we just don't like. If you have never had that experience of being subjected to the company of someone in this way, you are a rare and fortunate person. Because people are all different, and we are thrown into the company of all kinds of people, somehow we have to work out a system of learning to love these people—even if we do not like what they represent. You may think that it is impossible to love some people, because of the way they behave. But actually, there is a way of dealing with other people that has little to do with what they are or what they do. And this is a system that does not depend on the reward of good results.

The best way to get along with people is to love them. The greatest human need in the world is for love. This is not only what people need, but it is what they want, and what they respond to. I feel that I should warn you here at the outset, however, that to demonstrate such love is not always easy. At least, it is not easy at first—until one develops his ability along this line.

It is generally understood that a Christian, and especially a Truth student, is supposed to love everyone. But, I dare say, this injunction is not taken very seriously by most of us. We all have our likes and our dislikes among people. And so, the Christian injunction to love everyone is viewed by many of us (at best) as an impossible ideal, and (at worst) as sentimental twaddle. So, before any of the following suggestions are going to work for *you,* you must make up your mind that you are going to give them an honest try.

We are all aware that there are people in the world who do hateful things, and are not the least bit sorry for what they have done. And there are people who are just plain boring and unattractive. And these are the people toward whom we have no inclination to express love. I am sure that Jesus Christ was aware of that very thing when he said: *"Love your neighbour as yourself, and, A new commandment I give unto you, that you love one another."* Now, remember that Jesus Christ was a realist at all times. He did not profess ideals that were beyond the reach of human attainment. Rather, what he taught was designed to call forth the best that is in man—to enable man to express divine reserves that enable him to transcend his mere humanity.

In order to understand what Jesus understood about man, we have to become quite definitive about this word "love." It is a rather fuzzy word in the English language. In Greek, the language in which the New Testament was supposed to have been written, there are three words for love, each having a different meaning. These words are: Eros, Philia, and Agape.

EROS. Eros means being drawn to another person because of his attractiveness. That is, the object of the love is, in itself, the source of the love. The most complete fulfillment of Erotical love may be found in a happy marital relationship. But a person may quite properly feel Eros in varying degrees toward any number of persons of the opposite sex or of the same sex. It rests in a real application of the beauty, charm, merits, or talents of the person so loved.

PHILIA. In the second type of love, Philia, two persons are drawn together because of some mutual interest or concern they may have. They may not necessarily like each other, but liking the same things, they have an attraction. This form of love is sometimes very sad. You find it illustrated in many marriages, where the husband and wife not only no longer love each other, but they don't even like each other any more. But they stay married because they both like their home, or for "the sake of the children." The home or the children represent a mutual concern or interest, so they stay together through a Philia attraction toward each other.

AGAPE. With the agape type of love, we find something quite unlike the other two kinds. It does not depend upon the lovingness of another person, or upon shared interests. This type of love arises from recognition of the need of the other person for love, for interest, and for fellowship. This type of love has no "angle," it *"seeketh not its own."* This is the kind of love that is implied when we are commanded to love, not only our neighbours, but even our enemies. And when we think about it, this is the only kind of love that we could be commanded to give expression to. Erotic love cannot be produced in response to a command; and Philia love arises out of a particular circumstance and relationship, not out of obedience to law.

To give the sharpest definition possible to Agape, Jesus Christ chooses an example in which no element of Eros or Philia are mixed in. He says: *"Love your enemies . . . do good to them that hate you."* Quite humanly and naturally, you will feel negative, rather than positive, in your emotional response toward those who are "against you" or have tried to harm you. It will be difficult to feel a sense of sharing toward those who detest you. But this does not mean that you cannot help your enemy out of a difficult situation, feed him when he is hungry, offer him companionship when he is lonely. And this is the sort of activity that is called for in this very spiritual expression of love.

Obviously, there are some limits even to this kind of love. Since none of us are yet expressing the Christ consciousness in all of its fullness, our own time and resources are limited. Those persons to whom we are bound by ties of love and mutual interest usually have first priority. This is what Paul must have had in mind when he wrote: *"Let us do good unto all men, especially unto them who are of the household of faith."* In other words, there are those who would seem to get our special interest. Yet, if the goodness we show is limited to only those whom we like, then we are not really displaying the kind of love Jesus was talking about.

When Jesus Christ commanded, *"Love your neighbour as yourself,"* there was a lawyer who asked him, *"And who is my neighbour?"* At this point Jesus did not give the man a definition of who was his neighbour. Rather, he gave him a classic illustration. He told him the story of the good Samaritan. You know, in those times the Samaritans and the Jews would have nothing to do with each other. It was a feud that had been going on for five hundred years. But in the story, a Samaritan saw a Jew lying injured by thieves along the side of the road, and he took care of him. That is, he responded to the need that came to his attention.

There is an important consideration here. Day after day, our paths cross those of people in need: an unattractive girl perhaps working at your office; a man at a party who is withdrawn and self-conscious; a fellow worker who feels insecure in his job and needs to be encouraged. These are just a few of the opportunities that are presented to us almost daily—opportunities to respond to a need. It may not always be convenient to respond to these needs, any more than it was convenient for the good Samaritan to interrupt his journey and take care of the wounded man. But he responded to the need. And if we are to learn the craft of love, we must respond in like manner. The situations to which we respond may not be as dramatic as the one in the parable, but the need may be just as urgent.

You recall, in this story told by Jesus, that a priest and a Levite came down that same road, but they avoided the need, and crossed to the other side of the road. And they probably felt entirely justified in doing this. After all, this was not their affair, so why should they get mixed up in it? We hear about this same sort of thing today where, in large cities, people have been murdered while other people stood by and watched. They didn't do anything about it, because they didn't want to get involved. Interestingly enough, these people feel just as justified as did the priest and the Levite. And yet, love means involvement. Spiritual love means compassionate involvement where there is a need to be met.

If you have love in your heart, this automatically means that you must have some rapport with other people. Indifference is not love. Involvement is love. And oftentimes the grandest expression of love is toward people from whom there is no possibility of response. We must not extend some act of love toward a person because this indebts him to extend the same sort of act back to us. We must love because we have the spirit of love within us. And it is our spiritual nature to extend love.

Let me illustrate the difference between human love and spiritual love. Human love has its origin in one person and its fulfillment in another. That is, human love, coming from one person, must have another person toward whom that love is directed. When it is received by the other person, it is fulfilled. But spiritual love has its origin in the Divine Spirit within us, and its fulfillment in expression. You see, this spiritual love wells up within us, and we just express it. It doesn't have to be directed toward any one person. Spiritual love is simply and impersonally expressed. And it may be received by anyone who comes within its aura of influence; anyone for whom it may meet a need. Human love is often narrow and confined, while spiritual love is free and sweeping.

I am sure you have heard the old cliché: "If you are nice to people, they'll be nice to you." Well. there are at least three things wrong with that cliché. First, it may be true some of the time, but it is untrue enough of the time to result in cynicism. We often hear this cynicism expressed. "I've learned not to go out of my way to help people; they never appreciate you; people just use you," and so forth. Second, to give out in the hope of getting something back is a selfish quality of love. And it is not at all what Jesus had in mind. Pure Agape love means to give with no expectation of return. We cannot remind ourselves of that too often. Third, when we do good in the hope of changing an attitude toward us or gaining some advantage, the nature of the act is "written all over us." People will know what we are doing. Everyone is sensitive to love with an angle.

There is another approach to this idea that is most unsatisfactory. This is where some people do a good turn for other people they don't really care for, not because of the other person's need, but because it builds up their own ego and enables them to think better of themselves. This, in turn, poses additional difficulties. First of all, selfish love is unjustified. You see, all of the time, means and talents with which we may do good are not really ours. They are God's—on loan to us. And we are obligated to use a spiritually-borrowed talent in a spiritual way. This is a matter of (shall we say) divine ethics. Second, self-righteousness creates an intolerable twist in the personality, which makes us much less effective in our relations with others. So the act of expressing love has to be done right, or not at all. But there is really not much choice. If we give love its proper expression, our lives unfold like a beautiful flower. If we withhold it, we whither and die on the vine.

I don't mean to imply that the adequate expression of love needs to be complicated. Much to the contrary, it is most often adequately expressed in the simplest and commonest aspects of life. For the most part, we do not need to go outside of our family, or our neighbourhood, to begin to find opportunities to express love in a spiritual way. Here is a little verse that illustrates what I mean:

There's a gay and lovely lady;
She's the neighbour I adore;
She borrows three potatoes
And she brings back four.
Then I return the sugar,
A tablespoonful more,
And she says, "Well, here's a doughnut
To even up the score."

So, this is the nature of the craft of love—to love because it is your nature to love. You are created in the image and likeness of love. And love, spiritually expressed, is not concerned with the worthiness of the recipient. We just love because we must.

Perfect Balance

There is God and man, God the invisible, we the visible. God is the real of man invisible, we in perfect balance are the real of God visible. Both are one, and there must be balance. To be separated is sin, but in reality there is no separation—there is an assumed separation that is deadly. This separation is not knowing, ignorance. A separation we have taken on that does not belong to us. We have believed we are on our own. God and man cannot be separated because they are one thing, but if man thinks he is separated—as long as he accepts this—he is separated and misses his good. God is All Power, and man is the functioning expresser of this power.

In man God functions directly through the heart; feeling and knowing are the seat of wisdom and LOVE. Heart moves to the head as inspirations, ideas, needs, and desire. Heart is the God centre and the head, or mind, is the executive movement of the heart. Between these two there must be perfect balance. Off balance is a full head and an empty heart. We have gone off on the deep end intellectually, which would be great if we kept balance with the great Informer within.

We have filled our minds with information about the world, conditions, situations, outer causes, outer results, without an awareness that we are using the creative function and bringing these things into our life and world by our thinking and feeling. We must understand the cause as well as the effects. Unknowingly we are creating our world and affairs, and we ask, "Why are things the way they are?" With our heads so full of details we can no longer hear the inner voice that guides and balances all knowledge. The heart that should be warm and full to overflowing little by little dries up and becomes empty. The heart is the source, the head is the action.

In Jeremiah 2:13 it says, "My people have committed two evils. They have forsaken me, the fountain of living waters, and 'hewed them out cisterns, broken cisterns, that can hold no water." You may gather information from early morning until late at night, you can catalogue it with great care, but unless you can feel and receive directions from your heart, you are nothing. An empty heart produces a desperate human being. A full heart and active mind are a well-balanced being.

Modern man has put God aside, he has left the heart, the purest expression of Spirit. We have left the heart empty and inactive. We don't even trust our heart, but must find people outside ourselves to guide us. If your heart does not say, "Yes, Yes" to what others are saying, "Yes" to your own plans—don't follow, don't listen! Your heart should know first and your head is servant to the heart. We think of our own inner guidance as unreliable and weak, we say we haven't had experiences, but ONLY FROM WITHIN US CAN RIGHT DECISIONS COME. Outer knowledge is only a partial guide and must be balanced by inner feeling if we are to achieve fulfilling satisfaction.

Love: The Ultimate Power

I believe in LOVE. I believe that *love is the ultimate power for a power-conscious world.* I believe that Divine LOVE, beholding the potential for good in all creation, seeks always to draw that good forth, urge it forth, to meet needs as they arise. I believe this Spirit of Universal LOVE is truly *universal,* in and around everything, eager to cooperate in bringing forth greater good, that life may be more abundant.

As we meditate on thoughts such as those in the preceding paragraph, we find ourselves using the LOVE that is our true nature, working with LOVE, finding LOVE in action in the most wondrous ways. "Divine LOVE only doeth wondrous things."

In a shop, I was approached by a lady asking for change. She said she had tried the machine that was supposed to give coins in exchange for paper money, but it was out of order. I told her to try again, which she did; again with no result. I took the bill in my hand, caressed it, told it I loved it, loved the good that it could do. I caressed the machine, told it I loved it too, told it how it loved to be of service, how it would be blessed as it took this bill and gave the lady the coins she needed. I inserted bill, closed door, pushed knob. We laughed together as the coins came spilling into the lady's hand. This is LOVE in action. Childish? Perhaps. But ever-so-practical. And rather "heavenly," don't you agree?

An employee felt unjustly treated. She had been brought in from outside because of special qualifications. Others in the department seemed resentful, stand-offish. Even her supervisor was rough and unkind. She thought of leaving, but she needed the work and the money. Desperately, she sought help from a counselor, who pointed out her source of help lay within herself, through the wise use of her God-anointed LOVE-power. Whenever she thought of her supervisor, of her co-workers, she was to think, "I LOVE you. You are wonderful, for you are full of the goodness of God, put here to bless me and this place and this world." When they came near her at work, when she saw them talking across the room, she was to take hold of her thoughts and make them thoughts of LOVE. She did these things. Soon she felt free, found herself smiling at her fellow employees, greeting them happily, lovingly. Slowly but surely they responded, as their God-nature came to the surface, wooed into expression by our friend's persistent use of her LOVE-power. In less than a month she was called to the personnel department and told she was being given a promotion with a substantial increase in salary. Who had recommended her? Her supervisor. This too is LOVE in action. Divine LOVE, made practical.

It is not within the scope of this short article to tell you about the physical healings, the mended homes, the successful careers, the new beginnings, that I have seen come about through the dynamic power of LOVE in action. But there is no secret what LOVE can do. What it has done for others, it will do for you. Try it, beloved friend. And God bless you. I love you.

Transcendental Aloha

Teilhard de Chardin said, "Some day, after mastering the winds, the waves, the tides and gravity, we shall harness the energies of LOVE. And then for the second time in the history of the world, man will have discovered fire." It is through this LOVE that we find our future. Now that mankind continues to be more and more crowded, we can afford to take only those steps that lead away from isolation and toward greater LOVE.

The ability of men to LOVE appears largely limited. We are too much wrapped up in self. Our sphere of awareness includes only a few other people. The challenge is to transcend our religious, ethnic, racial bounds so that our LOVE takes on cosmic proportions. Stretch the limits of your concern to be aware of people the world over—many people, all people. Look beyond outer differences to the divine sameness of every person—the Christ within, the same God being born in him that is being evolved in you. Look at others with eyes of LOVE. Then you see them not as republicans, democrats, that religion, race, but as people. The age-old question "Am I my brother's keeper?" is resolved by the simple realization that "I am my brother's BROTHER." We cannot hate or fight our brothers. This is real LOVE—LOVE that transcends the normal bounds.

With the means of communication we have available to us today, we are aware of needs that people have almost as soon as the event happens. It makes a great difference when you read about something that happened months or years ago and when you are informed *as* the hurricane destroys, *as* the fire rages, and *as* the children go hungry. We are growing in our moral concerns. Each of us is becoming increasingly aware of cosmic proportions to our LOVE.

There is yet more to cosmic LOVE. Albert Schweitzer wrote, ". . . man belongs to man. Man is entitled to man. . . . Our age must achieve spiritual renewal. A new renaissance must come: the renaissance in which mankind discovers that ethical action is the supreme truth and the supreme utilitarianism. By it mankind will be liberated." LOVE that is real transcends our words to actions. It transcends the cosmic right back into our personal responsibilities.

LOVE that transcends its normal limitations must embrace the universe until it *comes back upon itself*. To really be in LOVE with mankind should open the door to be more in LOVE with any specific person too. Sometimes it is easier to LOVE humanity as a whole than to LOVE one's neighbour. One hundred years ago, a Russian landowner, Petrashevsky, recorded a remarkable conclusion. "Finding nothing worthy of my attachment either among women or men, I have vowed myself to the service of mankind." Cosmic LOVE embraces the distant brother and the close. Too easily we LOVE the far, and cannot get along with the near—the man next door, the children's friends, the mother with ancient ideals, the child with his radical concepts.

This is Aloha—Transcendental Aloha. A friendly spirit rising out of a sense of kinship with all people. Aloha encompasses the stranger, the enemy, and your own family. When you really LOVE all people, you can LOVE someone more fully. To really LOVE someone, you see your unanimity with everyone. The true spirit of Aloha is this kind of LOVE. Aloha transcends self to the cosmic and continues to embrace your own physical sphere of influence. This is our joy, our hope, our responsibility—transcendental aloha.

Brother of the Third Degree

My son, learn to love, for if you learn not here you cannot hereafter. Let your whole soul be ravished with the divine flame, but never for one moment allow it to be sullied by an evil thought, or lost in selfish preparation. Love your wife that you may the better love mankind; love your children that you may the better love all God's children, and then will the Universal love illuminate your mind and soul and bring you to all wisdom.

ɪɪɪ

I believe man is a temple of the Divinity, and that within him are Divine powers and possibilities. Man is not only a temple of the Divinity—man is the Divinity—Perfect man is God.

ɪɪɪ

There are three great steps in man's progress to perfection, and these are all included under the one word—self-control. Separately they are CONTROL OF BODY, CONTROL OF MIND, CONTROL OF HEART. Great is he who controls the body, still greater he who controls the mind, but greatest of all he who controls the heart.

ɪɪɪ

Knowledge is not to be communicated but evolved. Knowledge does not come from without, it comes from within. All your study of books and things is but to establish the instrumental conditions by and through which the Knower can break forth and manifest.

ɪɪɪ

Pure love is indeed eternal.

↑↑↑

Love so long tinctured by a thought of self, cannot be absolutely pure; pure love is universal, and includes all things, forgetting self.

↑↑↑

Then know what few men know, that every man is complete within himself, and nothing is there lacking if he will but search the depths. Love is but the soul's desire for a portion of itself, which it has lost, and without which its joys is incomplete.

↑↑↑

You must control your thoughts for every thought you think forms corresponding conditions in your mind and body. Thoughts are more powerful and potent than acts. Acts are but the expression of thoughts. Thoughts come first—we are built up of our thoughts, and we are surrounded by invisible powers and potencies created and given strength by the thoughts we think. It behooves you therefore to become able to guard the temple of your mind, and keep therefrom all things impure.

↑↑↑

God and nature are infallibly just and certain. Man has it in his power to go contrary to the laws which should govern his nature and by so doing, can, as it were, pervert nature and establish conditions not in harmony with divine good. Therefore in the world of men there is a certain amount of injustice, and men who identify themselves with this world are subject in like proportion to its uncertainties. But those who join themselves with God and work harmoniously with nature are never unprotected. It is a protection against all things exterior; only that within yourself can bring you harm.

↑↑↑

Now you may go—good thoughts and pure aspirations protect you.

↑↑↑

If man but does his full duty to man, he performs his full duty to God.

↑↑↑

There is one God, one man, one Brotherhood, one Truth. God is the infinite and all-pervading spirit, formless, immutable, eternal, and incomprehensible to all save itself. Man is an individual manifestation of God, in self-imposed conditions, a center in the Infinite Essence around which the Spirit vibrates, and through which it flows forth and reveals itself in the world of forms and things. The one Brotherhood is humanity, the sum total of all the individualized centers of the Divine Activity, which while apparently separate, are one in life and essence.

Truth is the full, self-conscious realization of God within its individualized manifestations, and the illumination that comes to each therewith. God comprehends all truth; and man, as God individualized, can comprehend all truth through God in him.

↑↑↑

Never do anything just to please somebody; do it because you think it is right, and remember that the less self there is in any decision, the nearer right it will be.

↑↑↑

A perfect musician can make only imperfect music upon a defective instrument, and likewise God as conscience and reason can make only imperfect expressions on imperfect man.

↑↑↑

The world cannot be saved by money or wealth, however much good it may do in isolated cases. Wealth and luxuries are not to be discarded except by those who cannot master them; while surrounded by wealth we do not allow it to consume our souls, like the avaricious men of earth. We believe in art, in music, in sweet perfumes and beautiful homes, but we do not allow the possession of such to blind us to the fact that everything here on earth is temporary and fleeting. We do not allow any magnificence to separate us from the poor; but we wish and long for the time when they can enjoy with us. Whether wealth is good or evil is determined by the influence it exerts upon the heart and mind. . . . Remember that everything on earth is good in itself, and only its perverse use evil.

Money and wealth cannot save the world. What can?

A reformation of man, and upbuilding of character, a purification and elevation of mind and heart—no external remedies or superficial palliations will do it. Everything objective is the outcome of that which is subjective. To change the visible you must change the invisible, and this can be done only through mind and heart.

↑↑↑

Never allow jealousy to contaminate your heart; keep it pure and good, for only thus will it be a fit place for the dwelling of the Divine.

↑↑↑

The man who seeks for truth with a selfish motive will never find it, for his desires will pervert his judgment and befog his reason. Truth is pure and undefiled and none but the pure in heart and mind can see it in all its beauty.

✓✓✓

Only the Christ within thyself can be thy saviour.

The Prayer That Is Love

I said to the Master,
"Tell me about the prayer that is LOVE."
The Master said,
"Tell me about the prayer that is not LOVE."
For if a prayer does not have LOVE in it, how will it get to the heart of things?

And if a prayer does not get to the heart of things, how will it change what has to be changed?

For things can be destroyed from the outside in. But things can only grow from the inside out.

And prayer changes things by causing them to grow.

God makes contact with us through our heart—always there—in the unconscious deeps of our nature. It is in the heart, the unconscious deeps, where the creative act always takes place.

Here is the secret place of the Most High.

Here is the house of the creative Spirit of life.

Here is the mansion of miracles.

Here is where the Infinite finds finite expression.

Here is where man and God are linked.

Here at our heart we have only to step a prayer's length to be in the heart of God.

Here at our heart we have only to LOVE to be in the heart of another.

But we have to LOVE.

There is a secret room at the heart of being where all hearts have contact and are not separate but one.

But only LOVE can enter that room.

And God is LOVE.

Here there is no you and I. Here there is only LOVE. Here if I be lifted up, I draw you upward with me.

For it is the God who is LOVE that is lifted and it is the LOVE that is God who lifts.

Letters of Myrtle Fillmore

For example, the Christ idea of LOVE is given us, GOD LOVE. LOVE unifies us with God, our source, and we know that we are good and true and fearless from within, because we let these God qualities well up from the center of our being. But LOVE alone would not enable us to keep our balance; it would draw us here and there without regard to what we accomplished. And here is where we begin to see the difference between the man Jesus Christ as we know Him, and the men who have fallen so far short of what we term goodness and real power. Jesus exercised all the God qualities we have yet been able to discern in a masterly way. GOD LOVE was expressed by Him; but it was supplemented and balanced by God wisdom, and power, and judgment, and will, and zeal, and life, and renunciation, and strength, and order, and imagination, and faith. LOVE drew Him to people; but good judgment held Him to a course of action that resulted in a success more far-reaching than any of us have yet realized.

†††

Be still. Be still. Be still. God in the midst of you is substance. God in the midst of you is LOVE. God in the midst of you is wisdom. Let not your thoughts be given over to lack, but let wisdom fill them with the substance and faith of God. Let not your heart be a center of resentment and fear and doubt. Be still and know that at this moment it is the altar of God, of LOVE; LOVE so sure and unfailing, LOVE so irresistible and magnetic that it draws your supply to you from the great storehouse of the universe. Trust God, use His wisdom, prove and express His LOVE.

†††

God is LOVE. But God is also life, and power, and strength, and substance.

LOVE is little more than affection and animal devotion, until other faculties are developed to the point of enabling the individual to see and understand in others that which is loved. Faith must be active; discrimination or judgment must help one to see the real and to understand that which appears perhaps unlovely; imagination must picture the God qualities in one's fellows and in one's environment that are lovable; understanding must keep the LOVE from becoming negative or selfish; will must hold one to a true course and to that which the good judgment indicates as best; renunciation plays its part in that it helps us to give up that which would hinder development. Strength must be recognized as from within and be so established that it supports every other faculty.

111

Jesus says that if we LOVE Him, we will keep His commandments. Remember what those commandments are? "Thou shalt LOVE the Lord thy God with all thy heart, and with all thy soul, and with all thy strength, and with all thy mind, and thy neighbour as thyself."

It is the Lord God within us that we are to be devoted to—to LOVE, unify ourselves with, be obedient to. Our own spiritual self must have our attention and LOVE and care and consideration. If we are neglecting our own spiritual development, our own health, we are not keeping this first and greatest commandment. And if we are not keeping it, we cannot keep the second.

So before we can truly pray, as Jesus says we should, and in answer to which He says the Father will do what we ask Him, we must learn really to LOVE our own spiritual self and do that which is best for us—and incidentally best for all others.

When heart and mind and body are filled with the consciousness of the LOVE of God and fellow men, we are prospering. That which we are prompted to do is accomplished. We are fearless and happy because we know that we are doing our part to establish and maintain God's kingdom in the earth.

The Grace of God Is Upon You

Because we are all sons of God, we are free to recognize and accept the grace, the LOVE, of God in the same full measure just as Jesus did. Because you are a son of God, you are meant to assume the same attitude, manner, and bearing, that you feel Jesus Christ Himself assumed in His earthly ministry. You are meant to act in the same manner as He, and you can, because the grace of God is upon you. You are meant to conduct yourself with the same dignity, having the same spiritual assurance you know He had, and you can, because the grace of God is upon you.

If something extremely difficult seems to be required of you, if you are faced with a trying situation, condition, or circumstance, set aside all doubts and fears right now, and for a few moments simply acknowledge your own divine sonship. Declare in faith: "God LOVES me. His grace is upon me, and only good can come."

Let the words "His grace is upon me" move through your thoughts; speak them aloud, then relax and accept them throughout your whole being. God's grace is upon you, upon your mind and its activity, upon your body and its functions, upon your life and affairs. God's grace is upon you now, blessing you, encouraging you, helping you, uplifting you, sustaining you, protecting you, guiding and directing you.

Wherever your duties take you, the grace of God is upon you. Wherever your duties keep you, the grace of God is upon you. However distasteful, unappealing, routine, monotonous, unrewarding your work or assignment may seem, the grace of God is upon you, and His blessings pour through you. However demanding, however filled with responsibility your appointment, the grace of God is upon you, and you are filled with new wisdom and confidence.

Because the grace of God is upon you, the dignity of Christ, the serenity of Christ, hold you poised; the LOVE of Christ keeps you gracious and compassionate; the competence of Christ leads you into success and satisfaction.

The grace of God is upon your hands as they serve, regardless of the capacity in which they serve. If your service seems menial and humble, the grace of God will transform that service into a ministry to the glory of God. If your service seems of great importance to the world, the grace of God will lend to that service a humility and beauty that glorifies not personality but spirit.

Know that the grace of God is upon every thought you think, every word you speak, every step you take; is upon your every action, decision, and movement. As you realise this, your thoughts will be clear, illumined; your words will be convincing, faith-filled; your actions will be spiritually significant, blessed.

Recognize, accept the wonderful truth that God LOVES you, that His grace is upon you as you grow and wax strong in spiritual expression. The grace of God is upon you this day, this hour, this moment. It is upon your body temple, upon your business, upon your home, upon your entire life, and you are blessed, blessed, blessed. The grace of God is upon you now.

The Yoke of Yesterdays

We must forgive and forget as we would that our own errors should be forgiven and forgotten by others. "Forgive us our debts, as we also have forgiven our debtors," is the prayer Jesus taught His disciples. It should teach us the futility of resenting trifling injuries, of wishing to "get even" with those who criticize or ridicule us. The Master's reaction to bitter injustice was "Father, forgive them."

To forgive as we would be forgiven is the very crux of our mental need. Forgiveness is essentially a function of the mind. It clears the channel through which Divine Mind flows into its individual outlets. Always remember this. To forgive is to remit, to absolve, to set free from the bondage of yesterday's yoke, to give something for something. The channel through which your forgiveness flows, to another is the same channel through which the forgiveness of others flows to you. If you obstruct its flow by denying it to your fellow men, you raise a barrier between yourself and God. As you would be forgiven, so you must forgive.

I am surprised to find so little understanding in persons who earnestly desire to be healed of sickness and poverty. They hold locked in their memories the buried microbes of dormant ailments, injurious to the mind and closely associated with their lack of health and supply. I find such people secretly brooding over past injury or injustice, resenting criticism and unkindness, or reproaching themselves for mistakes.

Before there can be any outward expression of healing I am sure it is positively necessary to heal the havoc that bitterness and ill-will create in the human mind. Perhaps it is, as many declare, humanly impossible to forget or forgive such wrongs as some have experienced. The human nature cannot accomplish this. It is the divine nature that extends mercy, LOVE, and pardon. From your human standpoint it is difficult, often seemingly impossible to condone an offense. Yet surely there was nothing of human nature in that prayer from the Cross "Father forgive them, for they know not what they do."

Forgiveness erases inharmony, anger, and jealousy, searching back of the petty faults and trivial mistakes of humanity until it beholds the true spiritual or Christ man. It indicates a removal of erroneous conceptions a "giving them over" for a like measure of freedom and peace of spirit. As it corrects mistakes, it cancels beliefs in evil and records only knowledge of truth. It springs from your soul, the innermost part of you. It is not genuine unless it totally erases every memory of bitterness. Its vision is broad; it sees beyond the petty faults of human nature to the actual spiritual self that is shining behind the clouds of limitation. It discovers the "Divine Son" in every individual.

You may be surprised to hear that first of all you must forgive yourself. If you are torturing your mind with thoughts of retribution for sins and shortcomings, you will remain bound until you make remission of your own faults by realizing the forgiving LOVE of the indwelling Father, who grants you the power to free yourself and others. When you have given your thoughts of discontent, resentment, faultfinding, hate, and lack for their mental opposites, the conditions of your life and your affairs are going to undergo a radical change.

Forgive your brother, yourself, your "fate," if that is what you call it. Forgive everything and everybody. Forgive, not once but even "seventy times seven." It is the only way to drop the yoke of yesterdays and remove the obstruction between yourself and freedom. Forgive and forget those things that lie in your past. Blot out of your memory the misery of your unhappy experiences. Demolish the old structures of worthless retrospection. Let the "first things" pass away, and behold "all things" shall be made new in your life. Give up your hatreds and criticism for LOVE and praise: your selfish gloom for joyous radiations of confident expectancy: your suspicion and distrust for faith in eternal goodness. Each one of these substitutes will accomplish rich results in your life.

Love Fulfills the Law

Prayer as a way of life is here to stay. Psychology as a way of life has been tried and found wanting. For years people turned away from prayer, as the impact of material science was felt throughout the world. We went through an age of unbelief. And we see the wreck it has made of human beings and the affairs of nations on every hand. But today there is increased worldwide interest in prayer. The need for spiritual help and guidance, for comfort and assurance is at an all-time high. Science has now proved the truth of many of the tenets of religion previously held only by faith. On many points of its own findings, and its former arguments against religion, science has done a complete about-face in the light of new facts uncovered. Science now agrees with religion on the power of LOVE and the law under which it works.

For one example, modern psychiatry has taught us the tremendous importance of LOVE in the health of the individual. One authority says that if psychiatry could be summed up in a phrase, that phrase would be, "Helping LOVE to triumph over Hate."

Dr. Karl A. Menninger, one of psychiatry's most respected teachers, speaking on the importance of LOVE reminds us that "it is the essential spirit of the prevalent religions of earth—Buddhism, Confucianism, Judaism, and Christianity—that one cannot live to oneself, but must love one's neighbour. And this is the same conclusion that we have arrived at in psychiatry."

Without LOVE there could be no safety for men on earth. And yet we see people all around us who either do not know about the law of LOVE or the power it exerts or they do not care.

But we do care. We are trying to make our dreams come true through learning to live in a circle of prayer. And LOVE is one of the parts of the creative power. It is number four on our chart. We need to study it, because the Holy Servant will bring back the answer to our prayer, even if accepting the answer destroys us. Our prayer will be answered, if we meet the law of faith, even though we ignore and go outside the law of LOVE to try to make our dream come true.

Let us be warned, however, that prayers outside the law of LOVE are black magic and fraught with danger. The practice of black magic is ages old. But even before the coming of Jesus the Christ bringing the doctrine of LOVE, men were not excused for using their creative power for violent, evil, and destructive purposes. There is a force in nature that acts as a cosmic policeman on the one hand and as a Holy Comforter on the other. It actually is another of the spiritual laws or powers which execute themselves. My students are taught to think of this one as the law of the Lord. For Lord means LOVE. And it works in that way. The Holy Comforter carries out the law of progressive good (good is LOVE) of all men at the base level.

Such a check and balance of nature, set up from the beginning of time, is utterly necessary if we are to have order and not chaos. The Holy Servant is man's helper, and must obey his word. The Holy Comforter acting as policeman and protector is higher than our Holy Servant, but only at the common level. In this way the one who transgresses the law of LOVE is found to punish himself. There is a way for the individual to specialize the power of the Holy Comforter for a private or a public good. For when we work with LOVE we are unlimited.

When we work against LOVE, we will run into the toils of the law of progressive good for all men. It operates silently and all the time. There is no way to defeat it. It forever trips up the tyrant, the dictator, the violent, the selfish, and the greedy. Like running water that clears the stream muddied by cattle crossing the creek bed, just so the law of the Lord is forever bringing the affairs of man back to the laws of LOVE. But only at the lowest level, we must remember. We have free will and are responsible for how we use it.

But we run counter to the law of the Lord, when we mistreat others. To try to outwit it is to try to do battle with the nature of the universe. In working with students, I found that more prayer projects are wrecked by infractions of the law of LOVE, than for any other reason—I dare say than for all other causes put together. The reason is this: it brings a sense of guilt. If we break the law of LOVE we do not feel worthy of God's help. We do not believe we will receive.

Love

One should make it a practice to meditate regularly on the LOVE idea in universal Mind, with the prayer, "DIVINE LOVE Manifest thyself in me." Then there should be periods of mental concentration on the LOVE center in the cardiac plexus, near the heart. It is not necessary to know the exact location of this aggregation of LOVE cells. Think about LOVE with the attention drawn within the breast, and a quickening will follow: all the ideas that go to make LOVE will be set into motion. This produces a positive LOVE current, which when sent forth with power, will break up opposing thoughts of hate, and render them null and void. The thought of hate will be dissolved, not only in the mind of the thinker, but in the minds of those with whom he comes in contact in mind or in body. The LOVE current is not a projection of the will: it is a setting free of a natural, equalizing, harmonizing force that in most persons has been dammed up by human limitations. The ordinary man is not aware that he possesses this mighty power, which will turn away every shaft of hate that is aimed at him. We know that "a soft answer turneth away wrath," but here is a faculty native to man, existent in every soul, which may be used at all times to bring about harmony and unity among those who have been disunited through misunderstandings, contentions, or selfishness.

Henry Drummond says that Paul's thirteenth chapter of 1 Corinthians is the greatest LOVE poem ever written. In his book based on this Chapter, *Love, the Supreme Gift*, Professor Drummond analyses LOVE and portrays its various activities. We quote:

THE SPECTRUM OF LOVE. LOVE is a compound thing. Paul tells us. It is like light. As you have seen a man of science take a beam of light and pass it through a crystal prism, as you have seen it come out on the other side of the prism broken up into its component colors—red, and blue, and yellow, and orange, and all the colors of the rainbow—so Paul passes this thing LOVE, through the magnificent prism of his inspired intellect, and it comes out on the other side broken up into its elements. And in these few words we have what one might call the Spectrum of LOVE, the analysis of LOVE. Will you observe what its elements are? Will you notice that they have common names; that they are virtues which we hear about every day, that they are things that can be practiced by every man in every place of life; and how, by a multitude of small things and ordinary virtues, the supreme thing, the Summum bonum is made up? The Spectrum of LOVE has nine ingredients, viz.

Patience—"LOVE suffereth long." Kindness—"And is kind." Generosity—"LOVE envieth not." Humility—"LOVE vaunteth not itself is not puffed up." Courtesy—"Doth not behave itself unseemly." Unselfishness—"Seeketh not her own." Good Temper—"Is not easily provoked." Guilelessness—"Thinketh no evil." Sincerity—"Rejoiceth not in iniquity, but rejoiceth in the truth."

Professor Drummond in his address on this chapter to Mr. Moody's students gathered at Northfield, Massachusetts said: "How many of you will join me in reading this chapter once a week, for the next three months? A man did that once and it changed his whole life. Will you do it? Will you?"

LOVE is more than mere affection, and all our words protesting our LOVE are not of value unless we have this inner current, which is real substance. Though we have the eloquence of men and of angels, and have not this deeper feeling, it profits us nothing. We should deny the mere conventional, surface affection, and should set our mind on the very substance of LOVE.

Charity is not LOVE. You may be kindhearted and give to the poor and needy until you are impoverished, yet not acquire LOVE. You may be a martyr to the cause of Truth and consume your vitality in good works, yet be far from LOVE. LOVE is a force that runs in the mind and body like molten gold in a furnace. It does not mix with the baser metals—it has no affinity for anything less than itself. LOVE is patient, it never gets weary or discouraged. LOVE is always kind and gentle. It does not envy: jealousy has no place in its world. LOVE never becomes puffed up with human pride, and does not brag about itself. It is LOVE that makes the refinement of the natural gentleman, or lady, although he or she may be ignorant of the world's standards of culture. LOVE does not seek its own—its own comes to it without being sought.

Jesus came proclaiming the spiritual inter-relationship of the human family. His teaching was always of gentleness, non-resistant LOVE. "I say unto you, LOVE your enemies, and pray for them that persecute you." To do this, one must be established in the consciousness of DIVINE LOVE, and there must be discipline of the mental nature to preserve such a high standard. The divine law is founded in the eternal unity of all things, and "LOVE therefore is the fulfillment of the law." Physical science has discovered that everything can be reduced to a few primal elements, and that if the universe were destroyed, it could be built up again from a single cell. So this law of harmony, which has its origin in LOVE, is established in the midst of every individual. "I will put my law in their inward parts, and in their heart will I write it." But before this fixed inward principle can be brought to the surface, man must open the way by having faith in the power of LOVE to accomplish all that Jesus claimed for it.

"The LOVE of money is a root of all kinds of evil." The LOVE of money, not money itself, is the root of all kinds of evil. Money is a convenience that saves men many burdens in the exchange of values. Primitive civilization used the cumbersome method of trading products without a money measure of value, while modern progress uses money continually as a medium of exchange. Money is therefore good to the man of sense perception; but when he allows himself to become enamored of it and hoards it, he makes it his god. The erasure of this idea from human consciousness is part of the metaphysician's work. Trusting in God, we have faith in Him as our resource, and He becomes a perpetual spiritual supply and support: but when we put our faith in the power of material riches, we wean our trust from God and establish it in this transitory substance of rust and corruption. This point is not clearly understood by those who are hypnotized by the money idea. When the metaphysician affirms God to be his opulent supply and support, and declares that he has money in abundance, the assumption is that he loves money and depends upon it in the same way that the devotees of Mammon do. The man who blindly gives himself up to money getting, acquires a LOVE for it and finally becomes its slave. The wise metaphysician deals with the money idea and masters it.

When Jesus said, "I have overcome the world," He meant that by the use of certain words He had dissolved all adverse states of consciousness in materiality, appetite, and selfishness. Christ is the Word, the Logos. Because the word is the mind seed from which springs every condition, great stress is laid on the power of the word, both in the Scriptures and in metaphysical interpretations of the Scriptures. The word is the most enduring thing in existence. "Heaven and earth shall pass away, but my words shall not pass away." All metaphysicians recognize that certain words, used persistently, mold and transform conditions in mind, body, and affairs. The word LOVE overcomes hate, resistance, opposition, obstinacy, anger, jealousy, and all states of consciousness where there is mental or physical friction. Words make cells, and these cells are adjusted one to the other through associated ideas. When DIVINE LOVE enters into man's thought process, every cell is poised and balanced in space, in right mathematical order as to weight and relative distance. Law and order rule in the molecules of the body, with the exactness that characterizes their action in the worlds of a planetary system.

DIVINE LOVE and human LOVE should not be confounded, because one is as broad as the universe and is always governed by undeviating laws, while the other is fickle, selfish, and lawless. It was to this personal aspect of the LOVE center in man that Jesus referred when he said: "Out of the heart of men, evil thoughts proceed." But in the regeneration all this is changed: the heart is cleansed and becomes the standard of right relation among all men. "By this shall all men know that ye are my disciples, if ye have LOVE one to another." We cannot enter fully into the Christ consciousness so long as we have a grudge against anyone. The mind is so constituted that a single thought of a discordant character tinges the whole consciousness, so we must cast out all evil and resisting thoughts before we can know the LOVE of God in its fullness. "If therefore thou art offering thy gift at the altar, and there rememberest that thy brother hath aught against thee, leave there thy gift before the altar, and go thy way, first be reconciled to thy brother, and then come and offer thy gift."

DIVINE LOVE in the heart establishes one in fearlessness and indomitable courage. "God gave us not a spirit of fearfulness; but of power and LOVE and discipline." A woman who understands this law was waylaid by a tramp. She looked him steadily in the eye and said, "God loves you." He released his hold upon her and slunk away. Another woman saw a man beating a horse that could not pull a load up a hill. She silently said to the man: "The LOVE of God fills your heart and you are tender and kind." He unhitched the horse; the grateful animal walked directly over to the house where the woman was, and put his nose against the window behind which she stood. A young girl sang, "Jesus, Lover of My Soul" to a calloused criminal: the man's heart was softened and he was reformed.

The new heaven and the new earth that are now being established among men and nations the world over are based on LOVE. When men understand each other, LOVE increases. This is true not only among men, but between man and the animal world, and even between man and the vegetable world. In Yellowstone Park, where animals are protected by our government, grizzly bears come to the house doors and eat scraps from the table, and wild animals of all kinds are tame and friendly. "The wolf shall dwell with the lamb, and the leopard shall lie down with the kid; and the calf and the young lion and the fatling together; and a little child shall lead them. They shall not hurt nor destroy in all my holy mountain; for the earth shall be full of the knowledge of Jehovah, as the waters cover the sea."

Beloved, let us LOVE one another; for LOVE is of God; and every one that loveth is begotten of God; and knoweth God. He that loveth not, knoweth not God; for God is LOVE. Herein was the LOVE of God manifested in us, that God hath sent hi only begotten Son into the world that we might live through Him. Herein is LOVE, not that we loved God, but that he loved us, and sent his Son to be the propitiation of our sins. Beloved if God so loved us, we also ought to LOVE one another. No man hath beheld God at any time; if we love one another, God abideth in us, and his LOVE is perfected in us; hereby we know that we abide in Him, and he in us, because he hath given us of his spirit. And we have beheld and bear witness that the Father hath sent the Son to be the Saviour of the world. Whosoever shall confess that Jesus is the Son of God, God abideth in him, and he in God. And we know and have believed the LOVE which God hath in us. God is LOVE, and he that abideth in LOVE, abideth in God, and God abideth in him. Herein is LOVE made perfect with us, that we may have boldness in the day of judgment; because as he is, even so are we in this world. There is no fear in LOVE; but perfect LOVE casteth out fear, because fear hath punishment; and he that feareth is not made perfect in LOVE. We LOVE, because he first loved us. If a man say, I LOVE God, and hateth his brother, he is a liar; for he that loveth not his brother whom he hath seen, cannot LOVE God whom he hath not seen. And this commandment have we from him, that he who loveth God LOVES his brother also.

My God Is Love

One of the statements of Truth taught to me when I was a child, and taught to many others at a very early age, is the easily remembered definition, "GOD IS LOVE." Without any strain of thinking whatever, the statement rolls easily off the tongue. Sometimes it carries a wealth of meaning. Sometimes it is given and received, merely as a familiar three-word phrase, to which no particular attention is given.

GOD IS LOVE—to some persons this conveys the impression that a God somewhere is constituted of an ingredient called LOVE. The form of this ingredient is to be imagined—solid, liquid, gaseous, perhaps. It could imply to some that this God somewhere has a heart full of LOVE for the universe and the people in it, but that the LOVE which is God need not be a part of them. It is the make-up of God, and may possibly not affect them at all. They may think: The God that is there is all LOVE. He can shed some of this LOVE in my life and affairs. He can enfold me with LOVE. He can influence me to LOVE others, and Himself. All this He can do if He so desires. He is a "something" associated with LOVE.

A completely different realization fills me when I personalize this statement. While I appreciate God as omnipotence, omnipresence, and omniscience, I draw closer to the divine Spirit and experience a singular thrill when I express in thought or words, "MY GOD IS LOVE." Immediately, I enjoy a strong sense of oneness. I accept the Truth that this God, my God, is the Lord of my being, and that He is all LOVE. Where is the origin of this God or this LOVE? Is it a spark that ignited within me at birth? If so, has it burned brighter or is it diminishing as the years roll on?

Is it a something that is there without any effort on my part and will it continue to be there, no matter what?

The more I think about it, the greater is the realization that

I am a contributory factor to my experience of God-power within me. My God is LOVE—all the LOVE that I generate within my being, for myself, for others, for the universe, is my God. The presence and the wisdom of God become real in me, and express easily through me, when I make myself a being of LOVE. I cannot afford to be unkind in thought, word, or deed. This would constitute unlovingness. MY GOD IS LOVE. All my good is built upon the foundation of this LOVE. My manifestations of peace, plenty, strength, and knowledge are greater experiences, because my God is then active within me. There is permanence and effectiveness in the presence of LOVE. I know myself as a being of LOVE, and I claim oneness with my God, LOVE.

This knowledge does not separate me from my fellowman. In my recognition of God as omnipresence, I know for every person that his God is LOVE. This thought unifies me in Spirit with all people.

The miracle of LOVE is not a power outside of me, trying to make entry and be expressed through me. It is a something within me, which I can allow to grow or not to grow. If I decide to let it grow, I can nurture it, cultivate it, and let it expand until it gains dominance in my life and my world. Absolute good is then the only experience in my life—Absolute Good is God. "He who does not LOVE does not know God; for God is LOVE."

My every thought, word, and action is a joyful improvement; my entire attitude pulsates to a startling, effervescing change: Strength, poise, calmness, and confidence come naturally to me as I hold steadfastly to and digest the Truth: My God is LOVE; your God is LOVE; our God is LOVE!

Love

Life is LOVE. LOVE is life. Life fulfills God through LOVE. LOVE fulfills God in life.

I prayed to God for LOVE. He said, "Take Me: I am yours."

I have worshipped God with LOVE. His Delight is my reward.

Spirituality is the all-embracing LOVE. This LOVE conquers man to make him conscious of his true, inner divinity, so that he can fulfill himself and can become a perfect channel to God's manifestation.

Try to LOVE humanity soulfully. You may say: "How can I LOVE others when I do not know how to LOVE myself?" I tell you how you can LOVE yourself. You can LOVE yourself most successfully just by LOVING God unreservedly. You may ask: "How can I LOVE God when I do not know what LOVE is?" My immediate answer is: "LOVE is the transforming power in our human nature. LOVE transforms our life of stark bondage into the life of mightiest freedom. LOVE cries for Life. LOVE fights for Life. Finally, LOVE grows into the Life Eternal."

We must LOVE God first if we really LOVE Life, for God is not only the Source of Life, but the Breath of Life. LOVE of God costs nothing, absolutely nothing, but is worth much, measureless.

As we cannot exist on earth without Life, so also God does not and cannot exist without His all-embracing, all-nourishing, and all-fulfilling LOVE.

Divine LOVE is sacrifice, and in this sacrifice, you are fulfilling God's will, consciously or unconsciously.

Divine LOVE is a flowering of delight and self-giving. Divine LOVE is the ever-blossoming affinity of souls. Divine LOVE is detachment; detachment is real satisfaction. Detachment and not possession should be the bridge between you and the object of your LOVE. Ascending LOVE, arising from the soul's joy, is the smile of God. Divine LOVE is all-embracing and self-existent.

LOVE teaches us: LOVE is our teacher. What do we learn from LOVE? Acceptance. We have to accept the world of ours. We must not reject it or throw it into the darkest abyss.

> Will you LOVE me
> Lord, if I come to you alone?
> Never. Bring quick
> With you the world, else I shall moan.

If you really want to LOVE humanity, then you have to LOVE humanity as it stands now and not expect it to come to a specific standard. If humanity has to become perfect before it can be accepted by you, then it would not need your LOVE, affection, and concern. You can and must LOVE humanity, not just as a whole, but also specifically if you realize the fact that until humanity has realized its supreme Goal, your own divine perfection will not be complete.

One has to use LOVE, not to bind or possess the world, but to free and widen one's own consciousness and the consciousness of the world. When your LOVE is vital, there is a conscious demand, or at least an unconscious expectation from the LOVE you offer to others. Vital LOVE lacking in purity is not only a stumbling-block but a dangerous limitation of consciousness that prevents our nature from turning towards the Divine fully and unreservedly. Ascending LOVE makes friends with the Everlasting. Descending LOVE makes friends with the fleeting breath of death. True LOVE enlarges the giver and brings him closer to God, even if he loses the object of his LOVE.

When your LOVE is pure or spiritual, there is no demand, no expectation. There is only the sweetest feeling of spontaneous oneness with the human being or beings concerned.

One must not try to substitute the heart's pure LOVE for the impure vital LOVE. What one must do is to bring the heart's purifying and transforming LOVE into the impure vital. You can consciously give pure LOVE to others if you feel that you are giving a portion of your life-breath when you talk to or think of others. Where there is oneness, it is all pure LOVE.

Be universal in your LOVE. You will see the universe to be the picture of your own being.

LOVE your family much. This is your great duty. LOVE mankind more. This is your greater duty. LOVE God most. This is your greatest duty, The Duty Supreme.

I know that I have to LOVE God and be LOVED by God, since I wish to live in the Beyond. I asked God what He does with His LOVE. God said that He protects me, He illumines me and liberates me with His LOVE. God asked me what I do with my LOVE. I said that like a child I just bind Him, my Eternal Father, with my LOVE. God cried with joy and I cried with gratitude.

I have LOVED Humanity. Humanity says, "No longer are you a stranger to me."

I have LOVED Infinity. Infinity says, "No longer are you caught by space."

I have LOVED Eternity. Eternity says, "No longer will you be caught by time."

I have LOVED Immortality. Immortality says, "No longer will death be able to bind you."

At long last I have LOVED God. God says, "My child from now on, you have bound Me in your divine embrace. You have bound Immortality, Infinity, Eternity, and Humanity."

Note: Sri Chinmoy is a great Indian spiritual master who came to the West in 1964. His centers are located in the U.S., Canada, England, Scotland, Puerto Rico, and Jamaica.

The Capacity of Love

The capacity for giving LOVE seems only to expand with use. For over three decades, Miss Martha Cooper taught the primary grade in the public school in my home town. Every year she welcomed to her heart thirty or so motley youngsters, loved and taught them all year and, still loving them, sent them along to the second grade. But forever after, each youngster had a permanent place in Miss Cooper's heart.

If you were sick she sent you a note; if you lost a relative she consoled you; if you won an honor in college she told you of her pride and pleasure; when your children started school, she was ready to LOVE and teach them, just as she had done when you were young.

"By now, you've loved at least a thousand of us. Do you still have enough LOVE left to stretch out and cover this year's crop?" I finally asked her one summer day.

She laughed. "If it were money, I'd not have. When you give away that, you don't have as much left. But LOVE is different. The more of it you give away, the more of it you get returned. You see, I think I always get back much more than I give—and that's how my capital stock keeps growing and growing."

Some years ago as Christmas approached, Dr. Milton Oberle, a kindly country practitioner in a little town just south of mine, found himself thinking often about his elderly patients, hoping they would enjoy the holidays and feel a little extra loved and cherished at that season. He liked and admired these patients, but unless he took some positive action, they would never really know how he felt about them.

Dr. Oberle had the typical crowded days inevitable in a successful small-town practice, but that year, during Christmas week, he made a special call on every one of these shut-ins and older patients—and to many non-patients, as well—to greet them, wish them happiness, and let them know he loved them and thought they were fine individuals.

He was a modest man, but he couldn't be unaware of the happiness he gave—and received. People were delighted with this proof that their doctor was actually concerned about them when they weren't sick, that he truly liked them as individuals, and that to him they stood for something more than arthritic pains, cardiac ailments, or troublesome digestive tracts.

Nearly all of us can express our LOVE and sympathy to the friend visited by tragedy or deep sorrow. But the technique of being truly outflowing is concerned with very simple everyday acts. It's the good word of praise that is passed along to the one whose name is mentioned—where it will cheer and hearten. It's the telephone call or note of congratulations when some friend or business acquaintance has had a promotion or other good fortune. It's the message of good wishes to anybody about to tackle a new job.

You are too busy for such considerations? Perhaps you are, but George, one of the busiest, most successful lawyers I know, is not. When I marveled at how he found time for his constant expressions of interest and friendship, he looked genuinely surprised.

"I never thought of those things as taking any time," he assured me. "They're just part of the day. In fact, I believe any day would seem interminably boring without them. Honestly, I feel buoyed up after a friendly phone conversation; I can work the better for it."

There is no estimating the business and social consequences of outgoing affirmativeness. Outgoingness can be polished and limbered if it has grown dull and stiff from lack of exercise. The rich rewards of one week of conscious cultivation of affirmativeness may surprise you. See what happiness and new interests can result for you next week from carrying through on the following six ways of giving yourself:

> 1. Go up to and greet either an acquaintance who doesn't see you—the person across the street or over on the other side of the store or somebody to whom normally you address no more

than "Good morning." Treat him as an individual with whom you associate certain interests. Let him know you are glad you happened to encounter him.

2. Write a note or make a phone call to some friend whom you have not seen lately but who has recently come into your mind. Or it can be to somebody who has just chalked up an accomplishment or has accepted some community responsibility. Make your message one of encouragement. Extend good wishes in a new job. Say that you got a lift out of his success.

3. Make an overture at getting better acquainted with someone you have met and liked but don't know well. Call him up and ask him to lunch with you. Don't be afraid to say you enjoyed being with him and want to know him better.

4. Pass along a compliment. When you hear somebody praised, remember what was said and give that somebody the pleasure of knowing it.

5. Tell your host or hostess you had a good time. Don't be content with having voiced your thanks along with your farewells. Phone later and reiterate your pleasure. Be specific about your enjoyment.

6. Show somebody a personal thoughtfulness that lets him know you have considered his individual tastes. If you have been entertained by a book that deals with the hobbies of somebody you know, tell him you think he would like it. If you have seen a fine photographic exhibition, mention it to a camera fan. If some homeowner has admired your dahlias, offer him a root when you do the fall digging.

These are simple, easy things to do. But it is just such expressions of friendliness, good will, and love for people that mark the affirmative attitude. We like it in others. It brings us greater joy within ourselves.

Why Not Be Nice?

Each of us will have several opportunities today to be kind, and the kindness we do today may stand out in someone's memory for a long time. If we have occasion to wonder just what we can do to make the world a little better, we should remind ourselves that at the very least, we can be nicer to other people.

The word "nice" has fallen into disrepute in some quarters; it seems to imply a kind of colorless, middle-of-the-road virtue without much force. But Webster assures us that "nice" is quite a nice word; one of the definitions of the word is "pleasing agreeable." And when you stop to think of it, you realise that when you think of someone as "nice" you think well of him.

Niceness is a quiet virtue, but it has a great deal of force and power. The nice people you know are pleasant, happy people, aren't they? Nice people are seldom bitter, frustrated, or negative in outlook. Nice people are the ones who work unselfishly in civic affairs, church, school, and other community projects. Nice people are the ones other people depend on. Nice people, we say, are "the salt of the earth."

This being the case, why shouldn't we make a deliberate effort to be nice? It's an effort we make all too seldom. Sometimes when we think of someone else as "nice" it comes as a little shock to realize that he stands out in our mind simply because he is better than we are. He performs services that we don't take time to perform, or he makes a greater effort to get along with others than we're willing to make. This fellow we regard as "nice" usually seems to get better service himself, in stores and shops, for example. Now, we are not particularly unpleasant to others, we tell ourselves, but somehow we often find something to complain about in the service we receive. Why?

The answer, of course, is that the fellow who is "nice" attracts good service; by his niceness, he makes others want to serve him better. To be nice to people we must LOVE them, or we will seem insincere. And actually, loving people isn't nearly so difficult as we sometimes feel it is. We LOVE our friends because we know them well enough to see that the good in them outweighs any shortcomings they have. What we must learn is that this is just as true of everyone we meet. If we look for the good in them, we won't notice their shortcomings nearly as much.

Finding the answer of harmony is not at all difficult, as long as we keep our "Spiritual battery" charged and connected. When this power source within us is operating at peak efficiency, we make friends easily, we breeze through our work effortlessly and accurately, we enjoy life to the fullest.

The Untapped Sources for Friendship

When we let this inner battery run down—when we become careless about our attitudes—life becomes dull and uninteresting, even unhappy. We become tired and grouchy and short-tempered. We criticize, we gossip, we spend a lot of time talking about how so-and-so is mean, or wrong, or dumb. We may lose some of the friends we have, and we certainly won't make many new friends.

I suppose there are few of us who wouldn't like to have more friends. Most of us, however, limit ourselves in this respect because we look for new friends among the people we know and like, people who share our interests. And these people, of course, are usually our friends already.

There is, however, a vast untapped source of friendships all around you: the persons you don't like. I mentioned this once to a friend of mine, and he said: "I know. And I know, too, that I can do a better job of liking people if I learn to see the good in others. But I can think of half a dozen people I meet frequently around town, at social affairs, and so on—who seem to me to be just downright unpleasant. Do you honestly believe I can learn to see the good in such people?"

I answered him by telling him about a conversation I had with my five-year-old son, Nick. During our talk I had occasion to mention that God loves everybody and everything. Like most children, Nick thought he saw a chance to poke holes in a "grown-up" statement, so he asked in disbelief, "Does He even LOVE gorillas?"

"Yes," I said, "God loves gorillas, too. He loves everything."

"Huh," said Nick, still unconvinced. "How does He get along with 'em?"

I thought Nick had a pretty good point there. How does God get along with gorillas—or with mean unpleasant people? The answer is a useful one, because we have to get along with others by using the faculties and ideas that God gives us. All of our human relations hinge on how we make use of His tools of understanding, patience, wisdom, and interest.

When you come right down to it, gorillas have something in common with unpleasant people. The powerful beasts, ugly and ill-tempered to our way of thinking, are gentle and affectionate among their own kind: naturalists who have lived near them in their natural state report that the big animals never bothered them or showed any signs of hostility. Apparently gorillas become violent and cruel only when harried by other animals or by men.

There is Good in All Men

In fact, naturalists say that there are few, if any, animals that are naturally mean and cruel, for the sake of cruelty. Can we say, then, that human beings are by nature mean and wicked, when animals are not? Hardly. And isn't it reasonable that we should give our fellow men, even the most cantankerous of them, as much consideration as we would give an irritated animal? Human beings develop undesirable traits and tendencies and attitudes as a result of stress and strain. They are faced with worries and anxieties and uncertainties (especially if they haven't learned how to find the answers they need), and sometimes their inner strength isn't adequately developed to keep them cheerful and pleasant. But the unpleasant traits that people have are not natural to them: they are basically and genuinely good, kind, honest, helpful, cooperative.

If you accept the idea that there is good in all men, all you need to do in order to benefit from this idea is stick to it, in spite of irritation, jealousy, distrust, and other negative emotions. Maybe you've been losing sight of the theory because it has been only a theory to you. Believe this, then: What has been theory is actually fact; the unpleasant traits and attitudes in some of the people you meet result from conditions that can be corrected.

The Priceless Ingredient

There is a priceless ingredient, available to all, that transforms any situation of which it becomes a part. It promotes healing, establishes peace and harmony, brings prosperity, dissolves fear, and fulfills every spiritual law in the universe. I am sure you realise by now that I am referring to Divine Love, the creative energy that is to govern the world tomorrow as man awakens to its power for good.

Not only will the poet, the songwriter, and the romanticist of the future be concerned with Love: the businessman, the doctor, the lawyer, the farmer, the preacher, the teacher, the craftsman, the homemaker, the ordinary and the extraordinary man and woman will be concerned with Love, realising that Love is their first order of business. The marketplace, the hospital, the school, the church, and the political arena—in fact all areas of human experience—will be known as ideal places for the addition of Love. Every transaction—commercial, professional, racial, international—is to be enriched and fulfilled by and through the power of Love.

Now is the time, here is the place, this is the event, to start adding Love to your life. You are designed to be the representative of Divine Love on the earth, in your work, your community, your world. You are as well prepared as anyone else to start the miracle working process of Divine Love in your life.

I add Love to everything I do, and I rejoice in the miracles Divine Love works through me.

I promote healing, establish peace and harmony, bring prosperity, dissolve fear, and fulfill the spiritual laws of the universe and my own being by adding Love to the transaction of my life.

Try This Experiment

Remember that "the proof of the pudding is in the eating." Here is a taste of metaphysical pudding that I suggest you sample. If you like it maybe you will want it for a steady diet.

This food is designed to feed the inner or spiritual man. This man in us must be fed, you know, and when he is well fed, all is well with the physical man. We are surrounded at all times by a bountiful feast of spiritual food that has been prepared by our loving Father, but we just do not seem to know how to get up to the table and help ourselves.

One of the most essential nourishing items on God's table is infinite Love. Many of us think of infinite Love as something so far above us that we cannot possibly appropriate it as we do food and use it for our daily needs. As a matter of fact, God's Love is closer to every one of us than we realise. It is so close that we need only think about it earnestly to discern that it is already in our heart. Therefore we need often to remind ourselves of the reality and imminence of God's Love.

For this purpose, I am suggesting a simple Truth statement for you to use. I think it will help you to become aware of the presence of Divine Love in a more definite way. Here is the statement:

"Divine Love is now working through me to adjust all the details of my life."

This is a short statement and easy to memorize. If it does not appeal to you at first, try it out anyway just for fun. Sit quietly and think about the wonderful possibilities of Divine Love. Write the statement down in your own handwriting and put it somewhere in your room where you can look at it occasionally. Then carry it in memory with you during the day, and when you have a few moments to spare, repeat it and think about its meaning. This will help you to get in step with the rhythm of God's Love.

As you say it over just imagine that the great healing prospering Love of the Father is enfolding you and protecting you from all harm. Realise that not only is Divine Love enfolding and protecting you, but that it is bubbling up within you, and flowing forth from you in loving, friendly thoughts and emotions to all the people that you meet, and to others at a distance that you know about but do not see.

Divine Love is not a static force. It is dynamic, and it will set you athrill with its power. "Divine Love is now working through me to adjust all the details of my life." Repeat this statement until it becomes a living, moving force in you and in your affairs.

Do not think of it as a charm or as something whose efficacy depends upon many repetitions, but repeat it with the conviction that you are stating a spiritual truth. Concentrate your thought upon the meaning of it, and as you do so the literal words will seem to open and unfold before your inner eye, and your understanding of the magnitude of God's Love in you will increase and amaze you.

When thoughts of Divine Love begin moving in your mind their effect will be seen in your affairs, creating greater harmony and order in your relations with others.

As you develop the spirit of harmony and Love within yourself, others will unconsciously be affected and harmonized. Conditions will also seem to become more friendly and thoughts of worry and fear will drop away from you, because you will be so secure in the consciousness of God's Love that you will not be disturbed by outer conditions. You will understand how David felt when he sang:

"I will fear no evil: for thou art with me; Thy rod and thy staff, they comfort me."

The trial Truth statement is meant to be a reminder to you of God's Love, which has always been and always will be with you. By repeating the statement and thinking of it as a living truth you will become more and more conscious of God's Love as an ever-present reality.

By dwelling upon this idea you will be able to quicken within you a warmth of Divine Love that will transform your life. Your affairs will move more smoothly than ever before, for Love is a lubricant like oil and will make life's machinery run more easily.

Keep your mind fixed upon the thoughts that God is of more importance than an earthly thing. That is, when you are meditating do not think about the conditions that need to be improved, but fix your attention upon the perfect conditions in God's kingdom. In this way you will hold the reality of the true conditions before your mental vision. It is faith in this reality that really counts for a harmonious, happy life. First must come the vision of the truth, and then it will work out in your affairs according to law, naturally.

Why not take time to make a thorough test of this little experiment, and prove the goodness of this divine pudding? Give it a fair trial, and I am sure you will find that it will open the way for many blessings to come into your life. Here then we have given a definite, simple idea that anyone can work on.

All blessings have their source in Divine Mind. Go direct to Divine Mind and tap its resources. This will not be a difficult understanding but a very simple one. We enter the kingdom of God by becoming as little children. Therefore with childlike faith and simplicity let us enter the kingdom of God's Love.

This statement is not the only way to find Divine Love, but since you must have something definite to use in bringing your mind into contact with the divine source of love, the statement may help you to find God's Love in your own heart.

Good Medicine

LOVE has been defined in many ways, but have you ever heard it called medicine? Believe me, it is. . . .

The flushed woman was desperately ill, raving in her agony as though living in a world far removed from this one. Her husband stood helplessly, unable to persuade any doctor to drive out at two o'clock in the morning. And then, breaking through the fog of panic, he called on LOVE—the eternal LOVE of this power we call God which can be invoked through prayer and in our thoughts and in our acts. Inviting friends to share their prayers of LOVE with him, he emerged from the engulfing panic to see his beloved for what she was—a creation of God, which is LOVE, as far removed from physical dominance as brightest day is removed from darkest night.

With a minimum of pharmaceutical medicine, the loved one emerged from the false world of agony into her real world of LOVE in a remarkably short time, for the true medicine would allow of no delay. Once God's omnipotence was acknowledged, the healing balm of LOVE blessed her rapid recovery.

The epilogue to this actual experience is a suggestion which is left for *you* to answer: Why need we wait for a crisis before we include LOVE, this most agreeable of all "medicines," in our daily diet?

The Way of Love

In your search for a happier, healthier, and more successful life, I am sure that you have often pondered over these words of my friend Jesus, and longed to know how you could put them into practice consistently and what they would do for your life if you could.

> Thou shalt LOVE the Lord thy God with all thy heart, and with all thy soul, and with all thy mind. This is the great and first commandment. And a second like unto it is this, Thou shalt LOVE thy neighbour as thyself. On these two commandments the whole law hangeth and the prophets.

One of the great obstacles to learning to LOVE God has been the picture of Him handed down to us, reminding us of a great landlord residing in splendour on his country estate while we, living for the most part in his decaying property in the city, make petition after petition for improvements which he might or might not grant, according to his whim. How could we LOVE someone so remote from us, whose ways and purposes seemed as mysterious, but who nevertheless held the power of happiness or misery, life or death over us? Such a relationship readily generates fear rather than LOVE. And, as for LOVING our neighbour or even ourselves, it is often difficult to find something LOVABLE from the purely human point of view in either.

But my friend Jesus painted an entirely different picture. He painted a picture of a God of Infinite LOVE who was Spirit everywhere present, who took pleasure in giving us our highest good, and whose place of abode was not in some distant heaven, but in the very being of each one of us, even our troublesome neighbour. And what's more, we didn't have to petition Him again and again—He already knew what we wanted. The way to bring forth this good that He had already provided was the way of LOVE, and we should start by trying to LOVE, not some cold and distant super-figure, but the warm, LOVING Spirit-potential within us to which we can relate more easily.

LOVE implies affection, and when we have a genuine affection for anything we are drawn closer to that thing, and it reveals its secrets to us. We can start learning to LOVE God, then, by seeking to draw closer to and to understand the divine potential within us. And as we do this we shall find talents and abilities previously hidden beginning to unfold.

LOVE implies trust, and the only way to learn to trust is by practice. We therefore have to practice placing more and more reliance on the guidance of the Spirit of God within us until we reach the place where we can say without reservation, "Not my will, but Thine be done."

But we shall accomplish even more by this switching of our attention from a super-power somewhere outside of us to the spirit of God within us. We shall begin to appreciate our own worth, and this will lead us to see ourselves in true perspective as unfolding children of God. A healthy LOVE of our own being will develop out of this new awareness of our true nature.

Furthermore, as we realize that what is true of us is also true of our "not-so-pleasant" neighbor, we shall begin to see him in a new light, a true light, and with that understanding will come the ability to LOVE him even while being aware of his human feelings, even as in our own case.

To LOVE the Spirit of God in our own being and in all God's creation will release undreamed-of forces for good within us. It will give us the consciousness that will attract only the highest and best to us, and it will ensure harmonious relationships with others.

And have you noticed something? These commandments that my friend Jesus gave us are inseparably entwined. You cannot truly keep one without keeping the other, and so it really doesn't matter which you start to work on. So begin with whichever you want, but please, begin NOW.

My Brother's Keeper

You notice that the murderer Cain, when asked about his brother, replies, "Am I my brother's keeper?" The whole point of this story is to stress the fact that you are your brother's keeper, and that anyone who questions it is speaking the language of Cain, the language of a murderer. The Bible lays down this principle in its early chapters, and it goes on to give specific details as to how we are responsible for one another. Throughout the Hebrew Bible we are commanded to help the poor and the needy, the widow and the orphan, to feed the hungry, visit the sick, clothe the naked, and to LOVE the stranger within your gates. We are given details of the rights of hired labourers— their pay and their working conditions. We are given details of the limitations of the power of rulers. We are given details regarding the defence of one's country. We are given details regarding honesty in commercial transactions, and a host of other regulations which are aimed at "social justice." Nowhere does it pander to greed and laziness, nowhere does it encourage defiance of properly constituted law and order.

Those people, therefore, who advocate subversion, who plot to overturn governments and society through arson, assaults, stabbings, shootings, and the like, such people are the descendents of Cain, and like Cain they should be marked men. They should be exposed so that all people can see them for what they are. Of course they will pretend to be working for the good of their brethren but on further examination it will be noted that they are only really interested in certain selected brethren, and definitely not in "the stranger within your gates." This is the difference between the religious approach to social justice and that of the anarchist or the atheist. Religion is concerned with reconciling all people, not setting one group off against the other. Religion is concerned with rewards according to the fruit of one's labour, and not grabbing what you can because of envy or malice. Religion is concerned with the spirit of sacrifice to assist one's neighbour, rather than the spirit of acquisitiveness to bring a neighbour down. Religion is concerned that the means used to achieve a righteous and moral end must in themselves be righteous and moral.

In fact, the difference might be summed up in two words— Jealousy and LOVE. The jealousy displayed by the murderer Cain divides brother from brother. The LOVE displayed by the life-saver Joseph reunites brother and brother. There is a wonderful phrase in Solomon's Song of Songs which reads, "For LOVE is stronger than death. Jealousy more cruel than the grave." Let us seek to avoid the cruel implications of jealousy and envy, and let us cherish the eternal values of LOVE. "Many waters cannot quench LOVE neither can the floods drown it." With LOVE deep in our hearts we can survive the waves of bitterness and lawlessness which threaten to envelop society, and that offering of LOVE, like Abel's offering, will surely be acceptable in the eyes of God.

When We Love

When we LOVE what we are doing, it is no effort to keep on doing it. This is why, if we would master prayer, we need to pray in LOVE and LOVE to pray. The prayer we make for ourself, as much as the prayer we make for another, needs to be a prayer of LOVE.

I doubt if we ever truly master anything we do not LOVE—whether it be a skill, a fortune, our own body and mind, an organization, an art, a science, a people, or an elephant.

But most of us rely on LOVE only occasionally. We do not have much faith that LOVE will work—except on those who LOVE us, our wife, or our child, or our friend. We have not come to the place where we see that the whole universe is the work of LOVE. Yet such it is. The tonic chord to which creation vibrates is the chord of LOVE. When we strike it, there is nothing in the world that does not vibrate in sympathy.

Love brings the beast to its knees, not through fear and force, but out of the urge to LOVE and be LOVED that moves the universe. When LOVE is in the driver's seat, LOVE is the beast that is driven. There is neither driver nor driven; they are one mind—the Mind of God, who is LOVE. One does not want to go where the other does not want to lead him.

LOVE is identification. I do not have to order my ears to hear nor my heart to beat. My ears hear and my heart beats—not because I order them, but because they are identified with me. LOVE foresees commands and supplies needs before the need is spoken.

I will not have to impose my will on another when we both are seeking to carry out the wisdom of God. I will not have to command another when we both are listening for the prompting of LOVE. I will not have to impose my will on life; for life will become not a coercion but a cooperation, a joyous enterprise in which every atom of creation shares; not one will be left out.

This is what the Master who was LOVE incarnate came to

show us: Life waits to give itself to us—it's powers and its treasures—when we give ourselves in LOVE. When we give ourselves in LOVE, LOVE with a few loaves and fishes feeds a multitude, heals a leper, gives back sight to a blind man, and in a matchless hour of giving even every remnant of self, rises triumphant over death and rolls away the stone from the tomb of all the sons of man.

The day must come when like the student in the story we will be going down the road and toward us will thunder the elephant. And we shall have only LOVE and faith in our LOVE. And we shall see, as the student tried to see, that it is not a beast that rushes upon us, but LOVE. And LOVE will kneel before us and lift us onto its back and bear us wherever we may wish to go. And we shall look about us, and all that we shall see is LOVE.

How God Forgives

In the Bible, light is the most oft-repeated symbol for the activity of God. The process is best understood in our oft-repeated illustration of the electric light bulb. Turn the light on in your room where you are. Instantly, the room is flooded with light as the electricity is converted into light in the bulb. Now, at any moment the light will disappear if you either turn the switch "off" or if there is a break in the circuit. The break is a "sin" and the punishment for this sin is darkness. The electricity did not create the darkness. It is not even aware of the darkness. We punished ourselves as a result of the break or separation and thus we have darkness. When we turn the light on again or repair the break in the circuit, the reward is light. It is not a special gift that electricity bestows upon us because we are good enough to make the connection again. The light is its own reward. Thus sin is its own punishment and righteousness is its own reward.

Sin is cutting ourselves off from the activity of God, and the punishment is the deterioration that always follows such separation. If I were to fix a rubber band tightly around my finger, in a few minutes the finger would redden and swell and then turn blue from lack of circulation. Before long, it would reach a danger point, and serious deterioration would soon follow unless I released the band.

What has happened here? I have stopped the flow of circulation with the rubber band, which cuts off the finger and the cells of the finger from the life-sustaining forces that flow in the blood stream. However, the reddened finger is not caused by the wrath of the life force in the body. It is simply the evidence of the absence of that force. And the life force in the body won't hold anything against the finger because there is no flow. The moment I restore the flow by removing the band, forgiveness is instantaneous. Life flows into the finger and in a few moments circulation is normal.

Habakkuk refers to God as "thou that are of purer eyes than to behold evil" (Hab. 1:13). This may surprise you, even disturb you. But it is vital to you that you get this point in your consciousness and never forget it: God knows nothing of sin, nothing of want, nothing of lack of any kind. This may be hard to accept—because we have a carry-over in our consciousness of the old idea of God who sits up in the skies and who looks down upon us, changing His attitudes about us, rejoicing in our progress, angered over our weakness or indolence. But when we expand our vision to contemplate the God of Universal Mind— God as Principle, God as Spirit—we see that God knows nothing of sin.

Does the principle of mathematics know anything about your mistake if you write two plus two equals five? The principle knows four even though you have written five, because the "two plus two" is an equation that means four regardless of what you think it means.

The tragedy would be if God did know sin. If God knew sin, He would be a sinner: for what Mind knows, it must be. Sin or mistakes are outside of the province of reality. Light doesn't know darkness. Light is. God doesn't know sin. God is. God is good, is omnipresent.

However, if God does not know sin, then how can He forgive sin, or how can man find forgiveness of God? How can man find release from his feelings of guilt? We find an answer in a beautiful thought found in the Old Testament, "Behold, I have LOVED thee with an everlasting LOVE." (Jer. 31:3). If God is LOVE, this universal essence that is as omni-active as gravity, then the statement is simply saying, God as LOVE cannot be anything else but LOVE. God does not hold less than LOVE for you no matter what you have done or haven't done, because God is LOVE.

Can electricity stop being electricity? Can light stop being light? Can gravity be less than gravity? Does gravity stop being gravity if you fall off a curb? If you are thrown to the ground, this is because gravity is at work, for that is what gravity is. Light is here when we open the window. Electricity is here at the flick of the switch. Therefore, God forever sees you as His beloved child in whom He is well pleased.

Let us turn again to the parable of the Prodigal Son. The father in the story is the divinity of you, and the prodigal son is the human side of you that forgets its divinity and experiences separation and ultimate "want." Thus the father is the son. When the son "comes to himself," he awakens from his ignorance of himself, realizes his innate divinity, and returns to his state of unity. He is received with open arms. There is no sense of guilt. The father doesn't say, "Now you are going to be punished for your sins." No, he showers him with blessings, and cries out, "My son who was dead is now alive again." The human consciousness has awakened to its true nature, and the very "hills clap their hands for joy." When the rubber band is released from my finger, the blood surges in with enthusiasm, and there is a veritable feast of "eat, drink, and be merry," as the cells come alive again under the influence of the life force.

How does God forgive? One answer may seem startling, possibly even sacrilegious. God doesn't really forgive sin. Or let's take a step further: God cannot forgive sin—no matter what the offense, no matter how great the guilt, no matter how much we may plead with Him for forgiveness. How can I get the forgiveness of electricity for disrupting its flow? How can I get the life force in my body to forgive me for shutting off its flow with the rubber band? By releasing the rubber band, by turning on the switch. And no one can do it for me. I must remove the band and turn the switch. And the force that surges through the finger and the switch—is it forgiving me? In a way you could say that it is. But all it is really doing is being what it is. Life can never be less than life, and electricity cannot be less than electricity—and God can never be less than God. God is LOVE even when I am filled with hatred. God is LOVE as the potential in me even though I am angry and bitter. The moment I release the bitterness, rise above my guilt, stop feeling sorry for myself, in that moment "God is LOVE" sweeps through me and loves me. But that is what it has always been. I just haven't accepted it.

Thus, in a very real sense, God doesn't forgive. God is LOVE. God hasn't held any unforgiveness. There is nothing to forgive in His sight, for "his eyes are too pure to behold iniquity." When the prodigal son wanted to come home he said, "I will arise and go unto the father." What did he mean by "arise"? "I will rise out of this limited consciousness, this faulty self-evaluation. I will stop living at the circumference of life. I will stop feeling sorry for myself in my poverty of mind and experience. I will accept the Truth about myself."

Did he have to go home and beg forgiveness? Actually in the story you will find him at first in a consciousness of begging. He rehearses a little speech that he plans to make to the father: "I will arise and go to my father, and will say unto him, Father, I have sinned against heaven and before thee, and I am no more worthy to be called thy son: make me as one of thy hired servants." But something happened to him on the way home. He dropped that servant consciousness—and perhaps there could have been no sense of union without that change. When he arrived home he said, "Father, I have sinned against heaven and in thy sight, and am no more worthy to be called thy son"—but nothing about "make me as one of thy hired servants."

It is notable that even though the son asks forgiveness, the father doesn't even acknowledge it. He simply changes the subject. He showers him with blessings. In our consciousness, we may feel guilty. We may be perfectly willing to take our punishment—to become "one of thy hired servants." That fact is we have already been receiving our punishment, for sin is its own punishment and righteousness is its own reward. In the attitude of contrition, the insistence that we become a "hired servant," we are engaging in words of futility. It is like trying to bargain with electricity to fill your room with light even though you do not turn on the switch. The moment you turn the switch you have light. The moment the prodigal really felt, "I will arise and go unto the Father" and could see himself doing it, he was instantly received of the Father and showered with that which the Father is—the divinity of his own nature.

The moment I accept myself in a higher context, in that

moment I have overcome, or come over, that which was the basic sin. That basic sin may have resulted in all sorts of secondary sins—but the basic sin was that I did not know who I was. The moment I come to myself, know the Truth of my innate divinity, my divine sonship, in that moment I turn on the light, and I let the flood of life and inspiration and intelligence fill me and thrill me—and I am transformed. I am forgiven, because I have forgiven myself.

"For if ye forgive men their trespasses, your heavenly Father will also forgive you. But if ye forgive not men their trespasses, neither will your Father forgive your trespasses." (Matt. 6:14, 15)

This is not saying that God is arbitrary and that He won't take the first step, but that you must show your sincerity by acting, and then He will act. This is simply a personalized way of talking about principle. It is difficult to understand the action of principle unless we relate it to things with which we can identify. This is why God is clothed in human form in the teachings of the prophets and of Jesus, and it is why we have gotten trapped in the concept of a God of the skies. God is LOVE and He can only LOVE you when you LOVE. If you want forgiveness, you must express forgiveness. There is no other way.

Talks on Truth

Make LOVE alive by thinking LOVE.

444

We may talk about the wisdom of God, but the LOVE of God must be felt in the heart. It cannot be described, and one who has not felt it can have no concept of it from the descriptions of others. But the more we talk about LOVE, the stronger it grows in the consciousness, and if we persist in thinking LOVING thoughts and speaking LOVING words, we are sure to bring into our experience the feeling of that great LOVE that is beyond description— the very LOVE of God.

444

LOVE is a divine principle and man can know it in its purity by touching it at its fountainhead. Then it is not tinged in any way by man's formative thought, but flows forth a pure, pellucid stream of infinite ecstasy.

444

You will find that the character of your whole consciousness depends upon how you think. You may have great LOVE, but unless you guide it with right thoughts, it will not build up a harmonious consciousness. LOVE poured through the heart of a mother, who has fear in her thought, shatters the body of a delicate child.

444

In the world we find LOVE so turned away by wrong thinking that it does not represent God. In its beginning it came forth from God, but it has been taken into "another country" of error thought and there wasted in riotous living.

✦✦✦

"And he stretched forth his hand towards his disciples, and said, Behold my mother and my brethren. For whosoever shall do the will of my Father who is in heaven, he is my brother, and sister, and mother." This is the LOVE of God in its purity, fresh from the fountainhead.

Wherever LOVE is tainted with selfishness, we may know that error thought has made muddy its clean stream, so that it no longer represents the purity of its source.

LOVE is the drawing power of mind. It is the magnet of the universe and about it may be clustered all the attributes of Being, by one who thinks in divine order.

Many who have found the law of true thinking and its effect wonder why supply does not come to them after months and years of holding thoughts of bounty. It is because they have not developed LOVE. They have formed the right image in mind, but the magnet that draws the substance from the storehouse of Being has not been set into action.

✦✦✦

"LOVE . . . taketh not account of evil." LOVE never sees anything wrong in that which it LOVES. If it did, it would not be pure LOVE. Pure LOVE is without discriminating power. It simply pours itself out upon the object of its affection, and takes no account of the result. By so doing, LOVE sometimes casts its pearls before swine, but its power is so great that it transforms all that it touches.

Always remember that LOVE is the great magnet of God. It is of itself, neither good nor evil. There are qualities given to it by the thinking faculty in man. Whatever you see for your LOVE, that it will draw to you because as a magnet it attracts whatever you set your desires upon. . . .

One with strong LOVE and the right focal idea may control turbulent multitudes by his silent thought alone.

When we speak of the power of LOVE, it should be understood that we mean power exercised through LOVE.

↑↑↑

You may trust LOVE to get you out of your difficulties. There is nothing too hard for it to accomplish for you, if you put your confidence in it and act without dissimulation. But do not talk LOVE and in your heart feel resentment. LOVE is candour and frankness. Deception is no part of LOVE; he who tries to use it in that sort of company will prove himself a liar, and LOVE will desert him in the end.

There is no envy in LOVE. LOVE is satisfaction in itself, not that satisfaction with personal self, its possessions and its attractions which is vanity, but an inner satisfaction that sees good everywhere and in everybody. . . .

The one who has made union with divine LOVE through his inner consciousness, who lets it pour its healing currents into his soul and his body is fortunate beyond all description. Instead of envying another he desires to show others the great joy that may be theirs when they have opened the floodgates of their LOVE nature. . . .

LOVE does not brag about its demonstrations. It simply lives the life, and lets its work speak for it.

LOVE does not seek its own. It does not make external effort to get anything, not even that which intellect claims belongs to it. It is here that LOVE proves itself to be the invisible magnet that draws to man whatever he needs. But instead of leaving this department of the work to LOVE, intellect sees what it wants and in its blundering way goes about getting it. Thus the real begetting power in man has been ignored until its true office has been forgotten and its power has been suppressed.

↑↑↑

This mighty magnet is a quality of God that is expressed

through man, and it cannot be suppressed by any outside force. No environment or external condition can keep back LOVE, when once you have firmly decided in mind to give it expression. The present unloving condition of the world is no bar to your exercise of LOVE; in fact, it is an incentive. You will know as you begin to make LOVE manifest how great a sinner you have been, how far you have fallen short of making yourself the man or the woman of God. This will show you by comparison how greatly you have missed the mark of the high calling that is yours in Christ.

✦✦✦

LOVE is in the world in a diluted form as affection between husband and wife, parents and children, friend and friend, but it can be made manifest in its original strength and purity by each man and woman's opening the fountainhead and letting its mighty currents stream forth.

The LOVE of God for His children is beyond description—a LOVE so tender and so deep that it cannot be mentioned in the same breath with the ordinary LOVE as known by the world. The great LOVE of Being is deeper and wider than the thoughts and the words of man have compassed since the beginning of language. It can be known only on its own plane, and man must awaken within himself the capacity to feel a mighty LOVE before he can comprehend how great is the LOVE of God.

But only the meek and lowly in heart may know the depths of the Father's LOVE. It is not revealed to the self-sufficient because they do not open the way through their own childlike, innocent hearts.

The Father yearns to have His LOVE felt by every one of us. He has given us the capacity to feel it, and He waits until we develop the LOVE faculty and open our lives to the flood of good that He pours out to us through His all-sufficient LOVE.

✦✦✦

LOVE, peace, and harmony, are the only remedies that count. "God is LOVE," and to live in God-Mind, man must cultivate LOVE until it becomes the keynote of his life. We must LOVE everybody and everything ourselves included. Some people hate themselves. Self-hate is destructive. You must LOVE yourself. Affirm the infinite LOVE as your LOVE, and you will find that there will be generated in your mind and body an entirely new element. LOVE is the cementing element of all things. You could not have an organism without the help of the cementing power of LOVE. LOVE is the magnet. You must have LOVE. You cannot live without it. Then begin to live in the thought of LOVE. Personal LOVE is part of the law, but divine LOVE fulfills the law. Centre your LOVE thoughts upon God, and you will find LOVE for your fellow man growing marvellously.

What is Peace

Peace is the goal of every man, and I hasten to add that peace is not a state of being in which nothing happens to us. Peace is one of the greatest, finest, and highest states of being. It is one in which it does not matter what happens to us. Peace is a state of mind wherein we know that something is sustaining us, and we know that we have a purpose. We know that there is a power and authority within, and all is well. We will not be shaken in our faith. Peace is an inner awareness of something within us, that we only feel, like the movement of an unborn infant in the womb of the mother. This which is within us grows and unfolds and envelops us. Peace is like a light that lights the darkest night. It may seem to be only a candle, but even a small candle in the darkness is a blessed thing.

Peace is a harmony and a tranquillity that we maintain when the waves of fear, anxiety, unhappiness, or shame wash up at our feet. Peace is a state of mind in which we look beyond that which the human eye can see. Peace comes when we move with and are conscious of the unseen. Peace is an awareness of the within, as well as the without. When man centres himself in outer things, gives his whole attention to the outer, he finds confusion, contradictions, and paradoxes that cause him to lose his peace. He becomes confused between that which is real and true, and that which seems to be. As man becomes aware of that which is within him, he realizes that his true life is not in the outer, but rather in his feelings, his reactions, his thinking, his longings. These make up life. He becomes aware that he lives in his own mind and heart. This inner peace that he finds within himself is a balance for all that is happening in his world. It is the inner peace within ourselves that is our power against every adversary.

It is important to walk up to all experiences with a feeling of quietness. Even though you may tremble and dread each step, you will have the knowledge that something will see you through and that it will work for good. Practice peace even if everyone seems to fail you. Even if your job is gone, your good seems to be slipping away, your loved ones have turned aside, and health problems challenge, practice peace. Stand in the middle of the kitchen, office, or street—or in any situation or condition—and bring your mind to peace. Power comes to the one who can hold his peace. This must not be an outer, seeming peace but a true being, an inner quietness. No "miserable inside" and artificial peace outside is of any use. It must not be hate with a face of peace, or a mask of pleasantness, but a peace that is sterling.

Man has lost his way into this inner peace. He has lost his peace. He has accepted conditions as they are, not knowing that the state of peace is absolutely necessary to the fulfillment of his good. When one is at peace, he is an open channel for all that is his by divine right. We all have what is ours by divine right, or we should have, for it is here for us.

Man looks at the world and its turmoil, and his inner peace is an answer to the world. Every man knows he should not lose his outer peace. To be able to maintain it, he must tap the source of inner peace. Our peace is important to the world. "Let there be peace on earth, and let it begin with me," should be the aim of every person. It is important to get up in the morning and fulfill the needs of life. We must do the serving, loving, and holding our peace just where we are. It will be each one of us in his own little place, believing and practicing peace within, that will be the real power in the world. We are the yeast in the lump. Let us realize how important we are to the peace of the world.

Let us dedicate ourselves to peace. Dedicate each moment of each day to the knowledge that you are the keeper of the precious power called peace. Peace has a great effect on man; it affects his life and vitality, his finances, his relationship to other people, his ability to work and concentrate. Your peace will affect your life, your body, your family, your business, and your world.

Peace is to be lived and enjoyed. Peace is always found in oneself. Peace is an inner quietness with which you meet each moment of life, always in control. Peace is a state of being in which you find full power and full joy. Try peace.

Single-Eyed Christians

There have always been intercessory prayers for world peace. In times of great crises, particularly world wars, very concentrated efforts are made, prayerfully (and otherwise) and a cessation of major hostilities has resulted.

In view of the seeming impermanence of world peace, the "outsider" could presume that prayer is not as powerful as it is chalked up to be and that religious organizations, (particulary Christians) should perhaps experiment with other methods, and test their effectiveness in the establishment and preservation of peace. There seem to be more crimes, more violence, more murders, more riots, more wars, and rumours of wars. The question may well be asked—"Are the prayers and intercessions for a stabilized and peaceful world really registering effectuality? Should the praying people cease and give up in despair? Perish the thought! It is sincere prayer that has thus far staved off greater deterioration of human morality. It is sincere prayer that has checked the volume and intensity of volcano-like eruptions of inharmony. What then is the lacking ingredient for a wholesale effectiveness of amity and concord? The greatest responsibility for the establishment of peace devolves on the millions of practising Christians, who may differ in form of worship, garb, and ritual, but who have no reason whatever to be deficient in unanimity in regard to the instructions of Him who was the Christ.

In so many places mankind has been taught, instructed, and encouraged to accept a two-faced God, a dual-minded personality, a schizophrenic creator. God is oftimes projected as a Being subject to outbursts of wrath, temper, and violence. The idea of God is sometimes mentioned as LOVE, in passing, but undue accent has been given to the presentation of a Being who in His fits of displeasure inflicts His creations grievously. He is sometimes represented as vengeful, and intolerant of mistakes and misdemeanors, and strikes hard and vehemently in the institution of corrective or punitive measures.

Surely this is not the God that Jesus Christ revealed to mankind, and it is incumbent on Christians in the act of emulating Jesus to totally accept the God He meant them to know.

> If ye then, being evil, know how to *give good* gifts unto your children, how much more shall your Father which is in heaven give *good* gifts to them that ask Him. (Matt. 7:11)

and again—

> Fear not little flock; for it is your Father's good pleasure to give you the kingdom. (St. Luke 12:32)

Jesus portrayed God as "Our Father," provider, protector, nourisher, sustainer, a loving Creator, and a Creator who is LOVE, and that is the manner in which He should be thought of, and acknowledged.

Jesus is quoted as saying "The light of the body is the eye: therefore when thine eye is single, thy whole body also is full of light" (St. Luke 11:34). Interpreted, this conveys that the illumination of the body is the understanding, therefore when your understanding is focused in one direction—the direction of seeing good, your entire world becomes illumined. When your understanding is negative, unbalanced, confused, and also focused on the things that are not of good (the ungodly) then your entire world is in chaos.

There seems to be then a need for universal single-mindedness. This being impractical, there is a need for the single-mindedness of Christians. Jesus expected this. He instructed His followers (Christians) to pray after a certain manner. First to acknowledge God as "Father," to affirm the same perfection and well-being in the sphere of the physical (our visible) world as is known to exist in the realm of pure ideas, the world of pure Being (heaven); to expectantly request a constant flow of spiritual and physical sustenance; to be assured that He will give us LOVE even when we make mistakes; in the same manner and proportion as we give LOVE for the hurt and unkindness that others mistakenly direct at us; to keep us free from destructive thoughts and attitudes and help us not to leave ourselves solely to revel in a world of materiality, mainly for the satisfaction of the human of us. And in experiencing spiritual fulfillment, and the accompaniment of satisfying manifestations, we will forever dwell in the realization that the Power and the Glory are of Our Father.

This confirms the utmost need for all Christians to dwell in the conviction of God as LOVE, WISDOM, POWER, and GOODNESS. Let this be the doctrine taught, and people will begin to understand that the onus of their adversities, afflictions, and inharmonies, begins with their separation in mind, (in thought and in act) from their Omnipotent Creator—GOD: FATHER: LOVE.

If we are to concede that this Creative Intelligence, this Infinite Wisdom is so unwise as to grievously afflict its creations, sometimes seemingly mercilessly, what type of behaviour ought we to expect from its creations? Is not the tendency of the child to emulate the pattern of its parents?

A great responsibility rests on those commissioned to teach mankind, or those who accept the responsibility to mold minds. If those who have gone on before contributed to the present dilemma, let us know that they did it unwittingly, and they are even now trying to correct the errors which were made, in good faith. To those who are now involved in the training of minds, let us try to be sure that we are not just as guilty, or more guilty than many of those who are the actual perpetrators of the incidents of inharmony and violence. It is not too late to unite in the promulgation of the idea of God, the Primary Cause, the Creative Intelligence as a Being that is LOVE. The results will be manifest. It will take time to undo the impressions that have been made, but the engraving will be in process in the newborn and young minds and with united effort and understanding the Christ peace which passeth all understanding will be established on earth. "With God (LOVE) nothing is impossible."

On His ascension Jesus Christ said to His followers (Christians), "Peace I leave with you, My peace I give unto you"

(John 14:27). If after nearly two thousand years, the idea of peace is not as evident as it could be, it is because He also left the idea of a God of LOVE, which the world has chosen not to accept.

Psychology reveals to us that any thought projected by the mass mind, brings into manifestation the like result.

There is absolute Power in the spoken word—the sincere prayer. There is a definite need for a greater number of persons praying with understanding. The greatest need, however, is for "single-mindedness" in the projection of the idea of God as a Father of LOVE. This is the price we have to pay for Peace. Forget the double talk and dual mindedness. Speak boldly everyone, everywhere in the unstinted recognition of GOD as LOVE, and let the creative, constructive, harmonizing Power of LOVE (GOD) take over and rule the world forever.

The Night the Hippies Prayed

I sat down and asked the group to do me a favour. At this point, I must explain that in all our meetings there had been no prayers voiced or even mentioned. Knowing the attitude of these young people, they would have laughed had I suggested anything like turning to God or praying. I meditated seriously for a moment on how I could get their support.

I had talked with those young people many times. I could feel their spiritual strength, even though they were unaware of any such potentiality. As I looked up at the group who had formed a circle, all eyes were on me. As I began to speak, my own voice sounded strange and far away. It was as though I was sitting there with the group listening to another's command.

Then, the words came slowly and deliberately. I said, "Kids, there is a person in the hospital standing between life and death. Now we are not trying to decide whether she is to live or pass on. I am not asking you to pray for her, but merely to give her your LOVE." I continued, "Just project your LOVE right over here in the middle of this circle, as though she were here. Keep pouring LOVE. Don't hold back—just give all the LOVE you have."

No words can express the powerful consciousness that was projected. A miracle was now taking place right in our midst. Time stood still . . . There was no time . . . Just a feeling of oneness among us, so strong that we were not separate beings. Patient, young people and myself all seemed melted into oneness.

Still dazzled by the strongest feeling of LOVE that I had ever experienced, I excused myself, and told the kids to continue their meeting. It was a ten-minute drive from the centre to the hospital. It was getting dark, and as I drove along the busy streets, these words rang loud and clear in my mind—"the night the hippies prayed." I found myself saying out loud, "Oh God the night the hippies prayed." Tears filled my eyes, and ran down my cheeks.

I hurried out of the car into the back entrance way of the hospital, and up the stairs to the intensive care ward. I knocked on the door, and a nurse appeared. She took one look at me and said, "We don't need you now."

She led me to the patient's bed-side and said, "She's all right. She's sound asleep. When we called you she was completely out of her head and started hemorrhaging again. We could not control her. About ten minutes after we called you she suddenly became quiet, and dozed right off to sleep. It was quite uncanny."

Looking at the nurse's puzzled face, I said, "You may think this strange, but I just left a group of hippie kids praying for this lady."

The nurse smiling said, "You'd be surprised at what these young people can do when they have a purpose. You tell them I said, 'Thank you.'"

Sky Prayer

A prayer came to me as I watched
the horizon full of clouds canoeing
across the sky:

"Father forgive me for trying
to make You small enough
to cram into the tenets
of any religious creed
Let me be big enough to admit
that You will never fit
Any pigeonhole built by man."

The Love Vibration

One reason we need to remind ourselves of the power of the "LOVE VIBRATION" and how to develop it is because, as Truth students, we are inclined to become very mental, and in our mental approach we can almost become cold and unloving, without realizing it.

A Russian nobleman, who took up the study of Truth many years ago, knew this. This man, Eugene Fersen, wrote: "The mind's eternal duty is to be expressed first in LOVE. This is the great lesson that mind has to learn—the lesson of LOVE."

There are those Truth students who get the impression that mind power is all there is; that if they just use mind power sufficiently, everything will come their way.

For a time, they may seem to be right. For a time they may produce tremendous results through the power of thought. The time usually comes, though, when they decide that mind power is not enough, and they begin to "spin their wheels" spiritually.

In your own life you may find this to be the answer at times: if your Truth no longer seems to be working for you, it may be that you need to use it more lovingly. Mind power becomes unbalanced when it is not used lovingly.

Developing the "LOVE VIBRATION" is the answer.

You can begin by affirming often, "God is LOVE." If the full force of this statement were realized in consciousness, a marvellous transformation would take place in man and his world.

As I related in my book, *The Prospering Power of Love*, some years ago during a financial recession, in bitter cold weather, the firm for which I was working experienced financial difficulties. Members of the board of directors had been depressed because of the weather, which seemed to be delaying the firm's prosperity. They were also depressed about the general economic conditions.

It seemed a hopeless situation until several persons working for the firm agreed to begin affirming together, at specific times, statements on the prospering power of LOVE. Each individual affirmed for himself and his own inspiration: "I am the LOVE of God in expression. I let God's LOVE guide, direct, and inspire me."

The statement used for the firm's prosperity was: "God's LOVE in us is drawing to us new ideas, new courage, and visible daily supply. God's LOVE in you is drawing to you new ideas, new courage, and visible daily supply."

The atmosphere of depression and hopelessness concerning the business situation seemed to lift. Continued use of the prayers caused all those involved to experience an uplifted state of mind. New ideas and new courage attracted visible daily supply. Within a few weeks the financial crisis had passed, and that year proved to be one of the most prosperous the firm had ever known.

LOVE is a certain kind of vibration. The "LOVE VIBRATION" releases a high-powered energy which is instantly felt and responded to.

Believing this, a businesswoman's club group decided to spend some time at their monthly meetings for an entire year affirming LOVE for the club and its members. This was to be their experiment in proving the power of the "LOVE VIBRATION."

Within a short time after the first meeting when they affirmed words of LOVE, several of these middle-aged businesswomen got married. One career woman had been widowed for twenty-five years, but she happily married and went off to southern California to live with her husband in a beautiful new home he provided for her. So many women in that club got married during the year of affirming LOVE that they had to reorganize the entire club. The leaders and officers of the group kept marrying and leaving town.

The "LOVE VIBRATION" works in both personal and impersonal ways. It releases more harmony and peace into our already established human relationships.

A housewife once went to her Unity minister for counselling. She felt that everything was wrong in her life: health, children, marriage, home, and finances.

Her minister declared words of LOVE for all her problems, and in their meditation period together, she affirmed for her husband, home, children, health, neighbours: "I LOVE you. I see the good in you. I have faith in the good in you. I bless you with all the good your life can hold."

She even got down to cases by naming her husband, her children, their playmates, her husband's employees. She spoke words of LOVE to them in her meditation; she blessed every troublesome situation in her life with LOVE.

When she arrived for this counselling session, she was depressed. But she was radiant when she left the minister's office. She was even more radiant a few weeks later when she returned to describe the transformation that had taken place. She said: "My husband has had a raise and he is giving that whole increase to me. He's been staying home in the evenings and we've had the neighbours in socially. It's wonderful. I've cleaned my house from top to bottom and fixed up many things that needed attention. I have more energy now. My husband says I'm starting to take care of my looks again, as I did before we were married. Something good is happening to the children, too. Everything isn't perfect yet, but it's so much better."

This woman proved that LOVE is a certain kind of vibration which is instantly felt and responded to when released through spoken words of LOVE.

It is certainly true that the "LOVE VIBRATION" harmonizes. This vibration can work in silence. You can let LOVE express itself through you toward others by silently blessing them, praying that the peace and goodness of God be poured out upon them.

Starr Daily, a man in prison who got his release after he developed the "LOVE VIBRATION" (as related in his book, *Love Can Open Prison Doors*), has told about the woman who came to him for counselling after he became a famous lecturer and writer.

This frustrated wife and mother told Daily about her troubled home: how her husband drank and gambled, how her teen-age daughter and son were giving her much trouble.

She said she had a degree in child psychology but it certainly didn't work on her own children. She lamented: "I've tried so hard to change my family, but I've failed. They resist everything I say and do."

Starr Daily quietly replied: "LOVE is not always trying. Sometimes it is ceasing to try. All you have to do is stop trying to "change" your husband and children. Turn them over to God with a confession that you are helpless in the matter. Turn yourself over to God, too. Tell Him you have given your family back to Him with no strings attached."

When the woman did these things, her husband became more thoughtful and his drinking and gambling diminished, finally ceasing. Her children began quietly sharing in the household duties, and became happy, well-adjusted young people.

Finally the whole family went away to a mountain resort where they enjoyed the first family vacation in years. The woman later said: "There is surely magic in LOVE. LOVE does things naturally and simply."

The "LOVE VIBRATION" also heals. *The Prospering Power of Love* is the story of a man who healed his body of a painful condition by placing his hand on the pained area and saying to it, "I LOVE you."

A busy career woman in Kansas City read of this man's method and it gave her hope. For some time she had suffered from a painful back condition. She had had an operation, but still the condition persisted.

She decided to place her hands on the painful area in her back and declare words of LOVE for it. The pain began to subside after her first words of LOVE, and finally it was gone completely. Later when the pain tried to return, she again spoke words of LOVE to that area of the body, and again the pain left. When I met this woman last year, she was beautiful and healthy.

A college professor read the same passage in *The Prospering Power of Love* at a time when he had a painful health problem. His doctor had told him he would have to learn to live with the pain that had been caused by a knee injury. In desperation he started placing his hands on the painful knee, blessing it and speaking words of LOVE to it. Instead of limping badly, he was soon walking normally again, pain-free. That was more than a year ago, and he has had no more difficulty with his knee.

Not only does the "LOVE VIBRATION" harmonize your life, and relax your body—even healing it—but it can also prosper you, even pay your debts.

In his book, *Prosperity*, Charles Fillmore has a chapter entitled "God Will Pay Your Debts" in which he points out the prospering power of LOVE.

In my book *How to Live a Prosperous Life* is the account of a lawyer who studied the book *Prosperity* and collected two large accounts by releasing the "LOVE VIBRATION." At the end of the year, in going over his books, he found two especially large accounts still due. He recalled that Fillmore had written, "A thought of debt, will produce debt."

He reasoned that as long as he believed in debt, resented debt, or attached the thought of debt to himself or others, he would remain in debt. To overcome such negative thoughts, and also to invoke the power of LOVE, the lawyer made a mental note of the clients who owed him large amounts. He began blessing their names daily, each one separately, and sincerely erasing the idea of debt attached to each one. In this way he released the "LOVE VIBRATION."

After he had been using this system for a short time daily, the two clients who owed the large sums settled with him on the same day, one of them mailing his check for the full amount from a distant state.

The "LOVE VIBRATION" also heals.

A little girl was disappointed when she realized that one of her playmates had taken a doll and cradle from her room. At first she was angry, and blamed various friends, planning to complain to her teacher at school about the theft.

But her Mother reminded her of the "LOVE VIBRATION." Together they declared "LOVE envieth not," that no one wanted her doll and cradle or anything else that was hers by divine right. That very night the doll and cradle were returned to their usual place in her room.

A woman once saved her house from being robbed, at a time when burglaries were being committed on all sides, by declaring these same words "LOVE envieth not."

A woman in San Francisco was suddenly approached by two masked men as she descended from a street-car one dark night. They said, "We're short of cash and we want the money in your handbag."

She replied with an affirmation: "God is my protection. There is nothing in the seen or unseen that can harm me, or make me fearful. I am overshadowed by DIVINE LOVE."

The masked man said to the other one: "Take her pocketbook. We've got to have it." As the other man snatched it, the woman said, "I hope it will do you some good." Then she added: "We are all God's children. We are brothers and sisters in the human family. If one has a need, the other should be glad to divide with him. I hope that money will be a blessing to you."

The two robbers looked at each other helplessly, shook their heads, and returned the pocketbook to the victim, whereupon she bade them "Good night boys." As she went on her way, she realized they had never even opened her bag.

The great thing about the "LOVE VIBRATION" is that it does not always have to be released through the spoken word. If the situation does not allow you that privacy, you can release it silently. God's harmony and perfect peace can be established by silently blessing the person or situation that needs LOVE.

You may wish to begin daily releasing the "LOVE VIBRATION" by affirming and meditating upon this statement for yourself: "God's LOVE. God's LOVE is doing its perfect work in me, and through me now. God's LOVE is producing perfect results in my life now. I am overshadowed by DIVINE LOVE."

For others you might wish to affirm and meditate upon these statements: "God is LOVE. I LOVE you. I see the good in you. I have faith in the good in you. I bless you with all the good your life can hold. Your life is overshadowed by DIVINE LOVE."

Choose Love or Perish

Our Planet has a fever.

Each of us, is the sum total of genes that go back to primordial days, and have altered by every event in the past. And, in addition, we are more than the sum of our parts—the whole is greater than the sum of its parts, and this proves the existence of God.

It is time that we grow up as human beings, and begin contributing more Love than hate to that sum total. If hate is more prevalent on earth than Love, our earth will continue to overheat. The frightening question is: Is there enough Love present in the world today to reverse the course of destruction?

Of course no one can answer this question definitely. But if the world ever needed a New Year's resolution, it desperately needs one in 1971. Each of us can contribute more Love by resolving not only to enlarge our own spiritual awareness but to give ourself away in service to others. There is not one of us who cannot help at least one other person by the extension of his no-strings-attached Love. We can share, if it is only a sincere smile from the depths of our heart.

Hate, fear, distrust, and prejudice are winning, at this writing, and can only be transmuted by each of us refusing to harbour such destructive thoughts and actions. "Each one help one" is no longer simply a nice idea—it is essential to our survival.

As students of positive thinking, we should be the vanguard of the movement towards Love. The admonition is devastatingly clear.

Choose Love or perish.

Because He Is Love

Who of us does not have times when he thinks he is not good enough to go to God for help? But God does not help me because He approves or disapproves of what I am doing.

God helps me because He is God. Because He is Life. Because He is Love.

God does not help me because I am good.

God helps me because He is good.

God does not help me because I deserve help, or Love me because I deserve Love.

Do you Love only those who have no flaws? And would you think that you can Love where God cannot? Love sees things perfect in spite of flaws.

I do not have to be perfect to lay hold of Love's perfection.

God does not answer my prayers to reward me because I have been good or deny my prayers to punish me because I have been bad.

God does not strike a bargain.

God does not work for pay.

God gives.

God does not wait until I give myself to Him to give Himself to me. He seeks me even when I flee from Him. And whither may I flee from Him who is everywhere at hand?

God has me in His heart, whether I have Him in my heart or not.

I do not have to be the most willing for Him to choose me, or the most capable for Him to use me.

It is not only good people God has used to do His good.

It is not only brave people God has used to win victories.

It is not only righteous people God has used to establish right.

So I hold out my heart and I pray, "God, whatever my heart may have felt, Love through it."

I hold out my mind and I pray, "God, whatever my mind may have thought, think through it."

I hold out my hands and I pray, "God, whatever my hands may have done, act through them."

For I know that God does not give His strength only to the strong, or His wisdom only to the wise, or His joy only to the joyful, or His blessing to the blest.

God does not help me because of what I am.

God helps me because of what He is.

God is Love.

The World in Your Heart

To say "Love is where you find it," is not to say very much. *Have you found It?* If you truly have, then you know It is the answer to all the challenge of life itself.

Let's become part of the world in your heart for a moment. Can you call back right now the feeling of your hand sliding into your loved one's? So simple a thing, but if you are both radiating Love at the time, there is an indefinable sense of sweetness in the very cells of your hand, a tide of happiness that sweeps through you. The Love is not the hands touching, but the stirring of a Presence that always waits in you. Have you found It?

Love is not "the real thing" unless it has become evolution of the Spirit. Love cannot grow you to stand tall in your soul, cannot go joyously before you, opening ways where there was no way, if you do not express It. "The Bible speaks of a mysterious sin for which there is no forgiveness: this great unpardonable sin is the murder of 'love-life' in a human being," Ibsen said. Did you ever think of it that way? If you bury over the Love that you are, with anxieties, resentments, and preoccupation with every passing appearance, how shall you be reached, even by that One who is Self of your self? You cannot, until you "come to." De-hypnotize yourself. That which lies outside, that which happens about you, has no power to dim "Love-in-you, your hope of Glory." The evolution of the Spirit is a mighty big concept but Love is equal to it.

It is impossible for you to be in any situation where Love is not, because you carry It with you. It is the lodestone for your good. But if you are not aware, of course you will not let It work. Oh, look homeward to your heart, stumbling, hungry one! In the world of your own heart is all the Love you could ever want, enough to heal your insecurities, enough to strengthen your body, enough to prosper your business, enough to bless others, enough to hush your longings, and bring you peace. *Believe, feel,* and *be.*

The Altar of God

One day as I sat on a high cliff overlooking the valley of the Allegheny River, I began to think of myself. And I found myself mentally repeating the beautiful words:

> When I look at thy heavens, the work of thy fingers,
>   the moon and the stars which thou hast established;
> what is man that thou art mindful of him,
>   and the son of man that thou dost care for him?
> Yet thou hast made him little less than God,
>   and dost crown him with glory and honor.
> Thou has given him dominion over the works of thy hands;
>   thou hast put all things under his feet.

And so I thought that if God could be found in the world of nature so significantly, how much more significantly could He be found in man—in me! After all, Jesus Christ said: "But, if God so clothes the grass of the field, which today is alive and tomorrow is thrown into the oven will he not much more clothe you, O men of little faith?" And thus it was that I began a most incredible journey—the journey within myself. That journey was to lead me to a most profound discovery.

I recalled that Jesus also said, "But when you pray, go into your room and shut the door and pray to your Father who is in secret; and your Father who sees in secret will reward you." It seemed to me that if one had to go to the innermost, secret place within himself in order to find and touch the presence of the Almighty, then the true altar of God must be at that deep, almost indescribable place within every man. This was my discovery: that the altar of God is within man.

This does not mean that God cannot be found in a mighty oak tree, or a sweet, wild blackberry, or in the cool waters of a creek, or in a pinewood altar. But it does mean that God is most accessible to man from within himself.

It is the spirit in a man, the breath of the Almighty, that makes him understand.

In the days and weeks that followed, I found within myself amazing reserves of peace and love and strength. I don't know whether or not it was physically discernible to others, but after times of reflection in my inner closet of prayer, I felt that I fairly glowed with what I experienced.

Still I felt that something was missing. There were other creatures in this world of mine, but my rapport with them was limited. Unlike Dr. Doolittle, I could not talk with the animals. I could appreciate the beauty of a multicolored bird, the agility of a squirrel leaping from one tree to another, the blithe speed of a doe. But it was not the same. I had plenty of people in my workaday world, but I wanted people in my world of worship, too.

I realized that I could no more stay in my world apart than Jesus Christ could have stayed on the Mount of Transfiguration. And I knew that, if I had something divine within myself, so did everyone else. I hadn't bothered to look for it in others. So I vowed to do just that. I reasoned that all men are created in God's image and likeness. And looking for this divine dimension in other people became the adventure that surpassed all others.

By seeking something divine in others, I have found that all people have an infinite capacity for LOVE—the same kind of LOVE that Jesus expressed to the hurt and hungry who came to Him. I came to know that people are courageous beyond all human bravery—that they have the same quality of courage that Jesus demonstrated at Golgotha. And I have seen in others, as in myself, deep wells of peace. Out of such experience and observation, I know that every person has these divine dimensions. There is a place within us all where we may touch the very presence of God.

I invite you to join me in the great adventure. Seek and find the true altar of God within yourself. Then acknowledge that same altar in every man. Once you have done these things, you will understand and experience the spiritual awakening of which the Master spoke: "Truly, truly, I say to you, the hour is coming, and now is, when the dead will hear the voice of the Son of God, and those who hear will live."

Teach Us to Pray

Every fear falls away as we enter into Thee and Thy glory of LOVE, and as we bask in the sunshine of LOVE, Thy LOVE, Thy never-failing LOVE.

✓✓✓

Thine harmonizing LOVE is mine, and I am restored to peace and health.

✓✓✓

DIVINE LOVE like a magnet, charges my mind, and prospers my affairs.

✓✓✓

Among people who observe and think, there is no question about LOVE's being the greatest harmonizing principle known to man. The question is, how to get people to use LOVE in adjusting their discords. . . . They fairly explode with indignation when LOVE, or some of its attributes, is proposed as a remedy.

✓✓✓

Paul says (1 Cor. 13) that LOVE is patience, kindness, generosity, contentment, modesty, goodness, good temper, truth, burden-bearing capacity, faith in everything, a hope for the happy outcome of everything, and never a thought of failure. These are some of the working parts of LOVE, but not all. The fact is that LOVE is fundamental in every activity of life, not only in the spiritual and mental but in the mechanical and physical as well.

Scientists describe gravitation as the force with which bodies attract each other. This definition holds good in the mental, in the physical, and for all we know in the spiritual realm. So what the physicist calls gravitation is one of the activities of LOVE. Withdraw for one instant the steady pull of LOVE from Mother Earth and we, her children, would be plunged into the depths of space and darkness. We should remember this when we are tempted to think that no one loves us. The spiritually developed soul gives thought and attention to these apparently invisible yet powerful forces, and by repeated mental contacts it unifies spirit, soul, and body in the one Mind, which sustains and unifies all things.

It is through this process of unfolding LOVE that great souls are developed. Men are not created great, but with the capacity to become great. Many factors enter into soul growth, some minor, and some major, but a soul never attains supermind power without LOVE. The reason why LOVE is essential in a great soul is that LOVE is the binding power, the factor so necessary to strengthening or fortifying the soul. Hate and antagonism are disintegrating, and they destroy the cohesion of the spiritual electrons and protons of which the soul is built.

The body is the precipitation of the soul or thinking part of man; if it has developed sensuality and separation, it must be redeemed by being unified with the soul, and this unification is accomplished through LOVE. When, like Jesus, we have developed LOVE for all things, even for our enemies, then the body and all its elements become plastic to thought, and we have all power in heaven and earth. The energy of light, through which creative Mind rules heaven and earth, is amenable to man, when his mind of LOVE synchronizes with creative Mind and he can say, "I and the Father are one."

111

In us who are followers of Jesus in regeneration, which engrafts upon the natural man the spiritual genius that causes him to develop superman power, it begins its work by inspiring us to do little things in LOVE. From this doing grows larger capacities until we attain the full stature of the Christ man.

111

We begin our overcoming by thought mastery. We begin to master thoughts of hate and force by first thinking and doing the little component acts that constitute LOVE.

111

In the silence when his mind is fixed steadily on God, and is functioning in the consciousness of infinite LOVE, the activities of man's brain cells synchronize with those of the very brain cells of the Master. Even the intelligent principle of the LOVE centre responds, and thus man becomes a spiritual radio with power to receive radiations from Divine Mind as well as power to broadcast them throughout his environment near and far, an ability that is limited only by the spiritual power he has developed.

111

All-enfolding God LOVE and protection free me from every thought of fear, and I am strong and well.

111

"Perfect LOVE casteth out fear." Jesus taught LOVE of God as the first commandment, and LOVE of neighbour as the second; There was no need for any other commandments. These two round out the law. Then the one and only effective remedy for fear and its ills is LOVE.

111

We have all been told again and again that we must LOVE God and our fellowman in order to fulfill the law of our being. Doubtless most of us have done this, and have had the experience of very pronounced demonstrations of peace and protection in our life, yet we do not have that consciousness of LOVE, which we feel we should have when we think of God. There must be a reason for this deficiency, and there is. We have thought of LOVE to God in terms of something of immense size, something that we must encompass as a whole, when the fact is that LOVE is a composite. It is made up of attributes, as is made clear by Paul in the First Epistle to the Corinthians.

According to Paul, LOVE is the name of a great variety of little commonplace activities of everyday life. Are you patient and kind? "LOVE suffereth long, and is kind." Envious? "LOVE envieth not." Egotistical and proud? "LOVE vaunteth not itself, is not puffed up." Are you temperamental? "LOVE doth not behave itself unseemly." Are you grasping and selfish? "LOVE seeketh not its own." Do you give way easily to your temper? "LOVE is not provoked." Do you behold evil as real and agonize over the evils of the world? "LOVE taketh not account of evil." Do you rejoice when disaster overtakes evil persons, and exclaim, "They got just what was coming to them"? "LOVE . . . rejoiceth not in unrighteousness, but rejoiceth with the truth." Do you patiently bear "the whips and scorns of time"? "LOVE . . . beareth all things." Are you open-minded and receptive to good, whatever its source? "LOVE . . . believeth all things." Do you anticipate the future with fear and forebodings? "LOVE . . . hopeth all things." Do you endure with trust and confidence in eternal justice? "LOVE endureth all things." The one and only remedy for the crosscurrents of fear is the restoration of the peace and harmony of life by LOVE and its combinations.

Love—The Great Resolver

Several years ago, I was working in Toronto, Canada, as an Insurance Underwriter. One of the fifteen women of whom I was in charge, Olga, was the proverbial "nasty piece of goods." Olga was one of many displaced persons from Europe, the victims of war, who had decided to make Canada their home. She was a handsome woman in her mid-twenties, and very bright of mind. However, she appeared to have an enormous "chip" on her shoulder. She was extremely rude to all and sundry, very uncooperative in her work, and seemed to hate having to be in her job. On the very first day of my joining the Company, she and I had a "run-in" that resulted in a silent, mutual rejoinder to hate each other's guts: The result, as you can imagine, was an atmosphere of extreme tension.

However, I have never been very good at hating, and so it wasn't very long before I found myself talking to my Unity Minister about the situation. She told me, "Denis, you don't have to LIKE everybody, but you do have to LOVE everybody." She went on to explain this apparent conundrum by pointing out that we "LIKE" people because of some outer reason, namely some aspect of their personality that we agree with or appreciate. However, truly "LOVING" someone is dependent upon our realizing that they are a Divine Being, a "Son of God" made in His very own image and likeness. With this explanation, she sent me off with the admonition to "find something nice about Olga, and express it."

She might just as well have told me to find something nice about a boa constrictor that had just entwined itself around my body:

However, because of my deep respect for my Minister, I decided to give her theory a try. So, in the days that followed, each morning in my quiet time, I would say silently to Olga, "You are the beloved child of God, and I LOVE you as such."

The first day after talking with the Minister, I waltzed into my office, looked Olga straight in the eyes and said breezily, "Good morning, Olga. How are you this morning?" Her response was a steely glare that I interpreted to mean, "Drop Dead!" The next morning I repeated the treatment. Still no positive response. So the third day I quit. However, that night I still couldn't rid myself of the feeling that my Minister MUST know what she was talking about, so the fourth morning once again I smiled at Olga and offered my "Good morning." She grunted. THAT WAS IT. I had broken the ice. From that insignificant grunt, we progressed until we forged a firm friendship. Some time later when I took a flight across the Rocky Mountains, Olga took a small coloured slide photograph that I had taken from the aircraft window, and by squinting into a miniature viewer, painted a magnificent two-feet square oil painting reproduction. In so doing, I found out that she used up several sets of batteries in the hours upon hours of work necessary to accomplish this "labour of LOVE." What a change from the Olga of old: And all brought about by such a small portion of LOVE as a "Good Morning; how are you!"

Later, in talking with Olga, I found out that she had always dreamed of becoming a teacher, but that with changing her country and her language, and being unable to finish her university education, she felt that this was now an impossible dream. As we talked, I reminded her that in Canada it was possible to become a teacher without having a university degree, by going through a teacher's training programme called "Normal School."

This particular conversation ended, and a few weeks later I left the Company to take up a position elsewhere. However, over a year later, as I was walking down the main street of Toronto, who should I see bouncing along toward me but Olga. She was positively glowing. Well dressed, with a spring in her step, and a ready smile on her face, no one could have guessed that she was the same morbid, snarly girl of such a short time ago.

After the usual greetings, I asked her, "What are you doing now?" Puffing up her attractive chest, she answered, "I am training to become a teacher. I'm in Normal School." The pride and enthusiasm with which she said it made me realize instantly that she had found her Divinely appointed place in the universal scheme of things. How happy she was. And how happy I was to know that my Minister's, "You don't have to LIKE everyone, but you do have to LOVE everyone" had produced such marvellous life-changing results.

Truly, LOVE is the great resolver—not only of personality conflicts, but also of many of the inner private conflicts that tend to make us intellectual and emotional cripples, and that so often force us to show to the world a self-image that is so very out of line with the true, spiritual Self that is, among many other wonderful things, the "Image of LOVE."

It Never Dies

LOVE knows.
LOVE cares.
LOVE grows.
LOVE bears.
LOVE takes.
LOVE gives.
LOVE loves.
LOVE lives.
LOVE never dies.

Real or Counterfeit

Love can be a wolf in sheep's clothing.

It can be a weapon.

If I act loving toward someone, how can they hurt me . . . they have to like me, or at least act as if they do. If my ruse fails, and they hurt me anyway, I am justified in withdrawing my counterfeit Love, for who would blame me when the other was so cruel and unloving as to return my Love with cruel words or actions.

When someone does something for you, you are obligated to that person. Counterfeit Love knows this and thus the personal ego can lift itself above others by obligating them to him . . . and yet never be accused of being a tyrant because nobody dares to question his loving acts and words.

There are two kinds of Love, counterfeit and genuine. The counterfeit is so subtle that it will fool the user. The best way to avoid the counterfeit is to forget all about Love entirely and concentrate one's attention on being a pure channel of God's activity, looking to and depending on God in every response to life. If one is successful at that, he can be sure that he is also loving—in the genuine sense of Love.

The Power to Be: Love

The feeling of LOVE is the spirit of truth that ultimately leads us into all the good that has been prepared for expression through us! All great religions unite in proclaiming that LOVE is the energy that fulfills the law, that completes our own divine nature. Modern researchers into the nature of man join the same chorus of LOVE. The feeling of LOVE "casts out fear," dissolves all feeling of separation and returns man to the feeling of Unity with his Creator. "God is LOVE" and the feeling of LOVE is unity with God. Unity with God leads to unity with all of His creatures. The feeling of LOVE is the unifying influence that links all creation into one great symphony of life. The feeling of LOVE is the light of the world, at work in our emotional nature, and as it deepens and expands through exercise our whole being and life are transformed.

↗↗↗

To feel LOVE is to feel God, and to feel God is to "practise the presence" of God, to share in the activity of God.

↗↗↗

The biblical statement "God is LOVE" is perfectly accurate. God is not a superman dishing out LOVE to you and expecting it in return. God is LOVE, and you are its instrument of self-expression. To LOVE God is to experience the feeling of LOVE—to let LOVE flow through you. As you let the feeling of LOVE unfold and grow naturally, you will come to understand and participate in its activity. You will soon be experiencing the action described in the following words: "The feeling of LOVE draws me closer to God, and I begin to feel that I and the Father are one" and

"The feeling of LOVE casts out fear, wipes out all sense of separation, and unifies me with my Creator."

↑↑↑

God is LOVE and in that LOVE there is no condemnation, disapproval, or fault finding. LOVE always welcomes its children back into the fold. LOVE always approves of its creation, regardless of the stage of unfoldment it is in. No matter how many eons, universes, incarnations, and civilizations humanity is away from its destiny, LOVE approves of it because it is only in an atmosphere of approval that creative action works constructively. In an atmosphere of disapproval creative action becomes destructive as it is in the world today. LOVE (God) approves of you as its child, or self-expression. It approves of you as the light of the world, the image of God. It approves of you as a human being, its vehicle of expression. It approves of you as a man or woman, boy or girl. It approves of you whether you are a doctor, lawyer, minister, businessman, worker, prostitute, thief, or in any other human role, because it is only in the atmosphere of approval that you are open to receive the light, the radiant energy of LOVE that frees you from bondage. The approval of LOVE never varies, unlike the sliding scale of human values.

↑↑↑

Does LOVE then approve of evil? No more than light approves of darkness, or health approves of illness, or life approves of death. LOVE is creative action, and it always clears the deck for improved and increased activity, an activity that must be expressed through each person. LOVE, the Father of lights, says in effect: "Son, I am glad you're back home. You've done a lot of living and have picked up some 'unforgivable' sins such as fear, a feeling of separation, condemnation, self-righteousness, and narrow-mindedness . . . so let's clear the decks. I approve of you for you are my son, and I know your potential. In this atmosphere, the feeling of LOVE, let all that stands between us go, and as we celebrate your home coming, the barriers you have erected between us will be swept away. You will soon be ready for a fresh start, and this time remember that I am with you always."

↙↙↙

"So have we come to know and trust the LOVE God has for us. God is LOVE, and the man whose life is lived in LOVE, does in fact live in God, and God does, in fact live in him. So our LOVE for Him grows more and more, filling us with complete confidence for the day when he shall judge all men—for we realize that our life in this world is actually His life lived in us. LOVE contains no fear. . . . Indeed, fully developed LOVE expels every particle of fear, for fear always contains some of the torture of feeling guilty. This means that the man who lives in fear has not yet had his LOVE perfected."

↙↙↙

It is only the feeling of LOVE that brings the peace that "passes" or brings understanding. The feeling of God in the heart surpasses any intellectual knowledge . . . "while knowledge may make a man look big, it is only LOVE that can make him grow to his full stature. For whatever a man may know, he still has a lot to learn; but if he loves God, he is opening his whole life to the Spirit of God," our delightful companion in the adventure of living, St. Paul, puts it.

↙↙↙

To LOVE God is to LOVE yourself, because you and God are one in LOVE. This is the secret of the first great commandment, and that is no doubt why Jesus said: "This is the greatest commandment. It comes first." This commandment comes first, not so much in order of importance as in order of execution. The second commandment is like it. There is no way to LOVE your neighbour unless LOVE is active in and through you.

ttt

Human relations is the most urgent area of human endeavour. Once we solve "human relations" in LOVE, our other problems will be well on their way to solution. Racial, religious, and social disapproval block the flow of LOVE that is the only energy capable of establishing peace and understanding on the earth. International disapproval and war are the sum total of individual attitudes; so put the stamp of approval on yourself and your neighbour and let the feeling of LOVE flow out to bring light into the world. The wisdom and good judgment of LOVE are operating through you.

To Justify Injustices

Some men are born into rich and happy families. They are brought up in a fairly secure world. They are well educated. They have happy families of their own and rear happy children. They survive in good health for sixty, seventy, eighty years, and at last die peacefully in bed surrounded by sorrowing and admiring survivors.

Other men are born half-starving and ill. They are brought up maimed in mind and body in a world of war and suffering. They are abandoned in their infancy. They are taught to cringe or bully. They are murdered in their youth.

How can we justify such injustices of birth?

Most of the time most of us accept our life as if it were just an accident.

We find ourselves healthy, unhealthy, poor, affluent, threatened, or secure; and we say, "It's God's will," or "It's luck," or "It's fate."

That God could will me good health and you ill health, me wealth and you poverty, me a long life and you an early death, I cannot believe. If God is, He is justice and He treats us with equal love and equal wisdom. God is law—or He is not.

The question has to be: Is the world run by law or chance?

Is there a reason why I find myself where I am and what I am—or is this just the working out of blind chance?

To believe that this world is the good work of a good God, we have to believe there is a reason why.

If LOVE made the world, there has to be a reason why there is an idiot child.

There has to be a reason why there is a race of men so insanely cruel that they torture and destroy whole races of their fellow men.

There has to be a reason why there is a natural catastrophe that wipes out a town—small children, young men and women, old and helpless invalids, all!

To believe that this world is the good work of a good God requires us, as I have said, to believe first that men are immortal. Then we do not judge life by its momentary-appearance; we know that one rainy, windy day is not all there is to spring.

Second, we have to believe that each person draws his own life to himself.

If this is a world where it is just good or ill luck that drew my life to me, then it is a meaningless world.

But if somehow I am responsible—if somehow my lot is a just one and law is at work in what my life turns out to be—if I am I am because this is what I have come up to, or down to—then it is a meaningful world.

Such a world as LOVE might make, such a world as Intelligence might make.

Is there reason to believe this might be such a world?

We cannot prove that it is such a world—but we can believe that it is.

We cannot prove the world is anything. Is it physical, mental or spiritual in nature? Is it the product of chance force or of LOVE and Intelligence?

There is no way to prove that man is immortal.

There is no way to prove he is not.

There is no way to prove that a man draws the circumstances of his life to him; there is no way to prove he does not.

But, to me, the only kind of world I can see any meaning in is a world where men are immortal and draw to themselves the circumstances they find themselves in.

And I find it impossible to believe that the world does not have meaning—even though the meaning may be beyond my power to comprehend.

We have to believe that this present life is just one episode in a life that began long, long before we were born and will end only long, long after we die—when we cannot say, but not before we have completed ourselves—or there is not a shred of justice in the whole sorry business.

You may believe that it is not necessary for there to be

justice—or what we would consider justice—in a world as vast and non-human as this appears to be.

Certainly God does not have to account to me for His actions. I cannot bring Him to the question—not because it is blasphemy to try, as some men think—but because I do not know how.

God gave me this mind to ask questions with—of Him and everything else—but my mind has only progressed to simple fractions, and to understand His answers I need the calculus, differential, integral, and infinite.

Now I can only guess at what God is like and what He is about.

But I believe that He gave me a mind capable of telling right from wrong and justice from injustice.

When I see people born with little chance to have any but a maimed and miserable life—spiritually, mentally, and physically—and others born into a world where they will have little chance to have any but a full and happy life—spiritually, mentally, and physically—it is going to take a lot of talking by God or anyone else to convince me that this is just.

A world where this little life we see is all the life we have, a world into which men are born into such unequal conditions— such a world is too unjust for me to believe God would have made it.

Therefore, I have to believe that this little life I now have is but an episode in my total life, which began before I got here and will go on when I have left here. And I have to believe also that the conditions I find myself in are conditions I somehow drew to myself.

The Irresistible Power of Divine Love

When I was a child, I heard a speaker say, "When your heart is filled with LOVE you will not be critical or irritable, but you will be divinely irresistible." This thought made such an impression upon me that I have never forgotten it. It has repeated itself many, many times in my mind and kept me from being critical and unhappy about inharmonious conditions.

"When your heart is filled with LOVE you will not be critical or irritable, but you will be divinely irresistible." To what do we wish to become irresistible? To the real, the true, the good things of life, do we not? By our ugly, cross, irritable, impatient thoughts we build up a wall of resistance to the good that we so much desire, and then we wonder why we are not happy, why we are not healthy, why we are not prosperous, why we are not making good in our positions. When we are in a state of irritability good cannot possibly be expressed in our lives. We have failed to let LOVE express itself, and without LOVE there can be no happiness.

There is the person who thinks that the world has treated him very badly, that no one understands him, that no one likes him, and that everyone is against him. You have heard persons say this. You have heard someone say that a particular person was trying to keep his good from him. Only one's lack of insight, his lack of LOVE and understanding, can make him think this for even a moment. The only thing that works against anyone is his failure to express the LOVE of God. When one cultivates the LOVE of God and is willing to let it express itself through him, he finds his life easily and quickly freed from the confusion caused by the belief that someone else wishes to harm him, to keep his good from him.

LOVE is an inherent power that, if allowed to be expressed in one's life, will transform every inharmony, will heal every disease, will transmute every negative condition into part of the harmonious whole. The results of LOVE are always good. But do not confuse sentiment and sympathy with LOVE. I am speaking of the purified, transcendent power of divine LOVE that expresses itself through you and me when we open our hearts and minds to it, when we recognize and encourage it.

If you feel a lack of satisfaction and harmony in your life, if your life seems hard and the way seems dark, it is likely that you are inhibiting LOVE. The first step in remedying such conditions is to forget about your personal self and to cultivate the irresistible power of divine LOVE in your life by giving something of yourself in a helpful way to someone else. In other words, cultivate the feeling of LOVE and be in expression that which you would bring into your life.

More often than we realize, the lack of LOVE in our lives is simply the lack of expressed LOVE. One may feel ever so kindly toward other persons but close himself in by not venturing to express any of his good feeling. The desire for LOVE is frequently the need to express LOVE toward others.

Let LOVE express itself through you toward others by silently blessing them, praying that the peace and goodness of God be poured out upon them.

If one wishes to clear up a misunderstanding, it is not necessary to speak openly, unless one is led to do so. God's harmony and perfect peace can be established by silently blessing the person or the situation that needs our LOVE.

The LOVE of God can do wonderful things for us; it will imbue our lives if we permit it to do so. It makes smooth the path that was thorny and hard. It changes our discontent into harmony and happiness. It dissolves tension and sends its healing currents through our body temple. It satisfies our needs and is the irresistible magnet that brings the substance of God into manifestation in our lives as our visible daily supply.

"When your heart is filled with LOVE you will not be critical or irritable, but you will be divinely irresistible."

Let us make this thought into an affirmation for ourselves, so that it can be a more positive help in our lives. "My heart is filled with LOVE, and I am not critical, irritable, or impatient.

I am divinely irresistible." We may feel a hesitancy in claiming to be divinely irresistible, because we associate the idea with personal attractiveness. But, after all, true personal attractiveness is dependent on something deeper than mere externalities. Unless there is depth of character and spirituality, there is no strength or drawing power in mere personal attractiveness. But when LOVE fills the heart it is reflected not only in the face but in the very life of the person; the beautiful becomes more beautiful, and the one who lacks beauty and regularity of features is so lighted up by the radiance of the inner glow of LOVE that he, too, becomes divinely irresistible.

To affirm, "I am the LOVE of God in expression," is helpful, too; for it is a starting point, and you will gradually and easily begin to transcend your human limitations. You will be surprised to find how easy it is to get the feeling of LOVE. LOVE is an innate quality in man, and it needs only to be called forth in order to express all its radiance.

Sometimes we make hard work of trying to express LOVE. We say to ourselves, "I just do not feel loving, and there isn't much I can do about it."

There may not be much you can do personally about it, except to be receptive to the feeling of LOVE. God is the source of all LOVE, not you. Therefore, if you just open your heart with the thought that you are going to let God's LOVE flow through you, it will commence to flow. It will flow through your body temple to cleanse, purify, and heal you. It will flow through your feeling nature to quicken a loving feeling and then commence its flow out into all your relationships with others.

As children of God we must be expressers of His LOVE. If we are not attracting the good that we desire in our lives, let us begin to think of ourselves as radiating centres of LOVE. We shall find that LOVE, the divine magnet within us, will change our world.

The Magic Presence

Grief for the death of a loved one is selfishness and but retards the greater good the loved one should be enjoying. Grief from a sense of loss is really rebellion against the Action of a Law that has seen fit to give another greater opportunity for rest and growth; because nothing in the Universe goes backward, and all—no matter what the temporary appearance—is moving forward to greater and greater Joy and Perfection. The God consciousness in us cannot and does not grieve, and the human part should know that as no one can ever get out of this Universe, he must be somewhere better than the place he left. In True Divine Love there is no such thing as a sense of separation, and that which feels a sense of separation is not LOVE. The sense of separation is merely one of the mistakes of the personal self, which it continues to dwell in because it does not understand the nature of consciousness. Where the consciousness is, there the individual is functioning, for the individual is his consciousness.

↗↗↗

If one really loves another, he wants that other to be happy and harmonious. If through so-called death, an individual chooses to accept a better chance for future expression, if there be the slightest spark of love, one should have no grief or desire to hold that loved one in a state of incapacity when he might go on to greater ease and freedom.

↗↗↗

Grief is a colossal selfishness—not love. Lethargy is selfishness—*not* Love and *not* Life. These sink the race into slavery, because they break down the resistance of the individual, by wasting the Energy of Life which should be used for the creation of Beauty, Love, and Perfection.

↗↗↗

Divine Love when consciously generated within the individual is an Invisible, Invincible, and Invulnerable armour of Protection against all disturbing activity. There is only one thing that can bring about Perfection anywhere in the Universe—and that is Divine Love. Therefore love your own Mighty "I Am" Presence intensely—and nothing else can enter your Being or World.

↗↗↗

There is naught in the Universe to say nay to whatever you desire, so long as it does not harm another of God's children.

↗↗↗

Divine Love is a *Presence,* and *Intelligence* a *Principle,* a *Power,* an *Activity,* a *Light,* and a *Substance.* When we command Divine Love to go forth and do anything, we are setting into motion the Highest Form of Action—the MOST POWERFUL FORCE.

↗↗↗

Love, Divine Mind, and Prana are ONE in the static or still state. Through the conscious action of the individual, Divine Love consciously directed, becomes Love, Wisdom, and Power in action. This is why Divine Love consciously directed to accomplish things produces such marvellous results. It becomes instantaneous and All Powerful as soon as the outer consciousness ceases to limit it.

↗↗↗

To have inharmony drop away from the body of affairs, the personality must let go of all thought, feeling, and words about inperfection. An activity that will always bring complete Freedom is for the student to pour out Unconditional and Eternal Forgiveness to everybody and everything. This does what nothing else can do to free everyone, as well as the person who sends it out. When Forgiveness is sincere, the individual will find his world reordered, as if by magic, and filled with every good thing; but remember that unless a discord is forgotten, it is not forgiven, because you cannot loose it or release yourself from it until it is out of your consciousness. So long as you remember an injustice, or a disturbed feeling, you have not forgiven either the person, or the condition.

111

By accepting and keeping the attention on the "I AM" Presence, the individual can at any moment draw all good into the outer use of the personality. Thus he can call forth into his Being and world all the good he desires, but the greatest Power that this Truth places at the command of the personal self is the use of Divine Love, as a "Presence" which goes before it, and adjusts all outer activities, solves all human problems and reveals the Perfection that must come forth upon earth. Divine Love, being the Heart of Infinity, and of the Individual is an ever-flowing Intelligent Flame that releases Energy, Wisdom, Power, and Substance without limit. It will release Boundless Blessings to all who will harmonize their own personalities long enough to let IT come through. Divine Love is the Reservoir of Life, and the Treasure Chest of the Universe.

111

Love serves, because it is the nature of Love to give, and It is not concerned with, nor does It expect, acknowledgment of Its Gifts. . . . Just try to become the Love that does not wish to possess, for then Love is truly Divine.

111

Many people carry a feeling of personal grudge against Life, blaming It for suffering and failures, when even a very small amount of gratitude and Love poured out to the "I AM" Presence within each human Heart, would transmute every discord into Peace and Love, releasing the Perfection of Life into the outer activity of the individual. Human beings find plenty of time to love dogs, cats, food, clothes, money, diamonds, people, and a thousand and one things; but it is very rarely that an individual takes even five minutes out of a Lifetime to love His own Divinity, yet he is using every second Its Life and Energy by which to enjoy these things. . . . It is not that we should not pour out Love to things in the outer activity, but we should certainly love the Divinity Within first, and more than any outer thing or personality. It is this very Life and Consciousness by which we exist. Happiness cannot exist except when Love is pouring out. This is Life's Law. When people are loving something or somebody, they are happy.

✓✓✓

To send out Divine Love without limit all the time is the whole of the Law applied. Divine Love is a Feeling, an actual Ray of Light which flows out from the Flame within the Heart. It can be sent so powerfully that this Ray of Light Substance is both visible and tangible. It is the most Invincible Power of the Universe. Use It, Beloved Ones, without limit and nothing is impossible to you.

✓✓✓

The personality cannot be permanently harmonious except it be kept filled with Divine Love consciously generated.

✓✓✓

The outer world likes to flatter its vanity by the feeling that it has the ability to accomplish great things; but as far as the

Control and Perfection of the feelings are concerned, the outer world is still in a savage state. Human Beings sting others as well as themselves through vicious feelings, just as surely as does the scorpion. The predominant feeling in our modern world is terrifically vicious, when personalities are opposing and criticizing those who disagree with them. So-called civilized people commit murder every day of the week, through sending out angry and irritated feelings that kill the higher impulses in others. . . . Until the individual understands the need of Self-Control, in regard to his feelings—in the waking consciousness—it is impossible to maintain any permanent forward movement of a constructive nature. All accomplishment that is not attained through the Feeling of Divine Love, is but temporary, for Divine Love alone is the Way to Permanent Perfection.

↑↑↑

So mankind need no longer fool itself with the idea that it can continue to generate destructive feelings and survive. . . . There is no evil anywhere on this earth or any other, except that which human beings have generated themselves, some time, somewhere. Most of it has been done through ignorance, but a great deal has been done wilfully by those who ought to know better and who are fully aware of their wrong-doing. The individual who uses his intellect to foster destructive activities in the new cycle, into which we have recently entered, must face his own destruction for its recoil is inevitable.

↑↑↑

The Great All Wise Creator of Perfect Form, everywhere throughout space, builds those forms according to the Pattern of Perfection, which is another name for the Law of Divine Love. This always means the orderly, harmonious way of attraction. The feeling of fear, doubt, etc. is a rate of vibration which shatters form and scatters substance, hence is diametrically opposed to Love, Harmony, and Order.

Divine Love Is the Catalyst

A distraught young mother of two little boys came to the centre for counselling. She had problems just as most of us do at one time or another.

Her children were "driving her out of her mind," and her husband was informing her daily that she was "absolutely impossible to live with and was driving him out of his."

She talked copiously, which is always most helpful to get a problem out into the open, to let it go.

Suffice to say, there was prayer for light, and later we agreed that what was needed was a great big dose of DIVINE LOVE. "DIVINE LOVE," I told her, "is beyond all emotions or passion; it is a power, a spiritual power that attracts to you all that is good for you while, at the same time, repelling all that is not good for you."

Having agreed that DIVINE LOVE is the essential, we created the following affirmative prayer. "DIVINE LOVE is the ruling power in my life, in my home, in my marriage, between me and my husband and our children. LOVING understanding, peace, order, and harmony are now established. Thank you, God."

We affirmed this prayer several times. When she left, she took a copy with her and promised she would use it faithfully— would repeat it until, when she ceased, it would repeat itself in her consciousness. She also promised to follow her hunches—a colloquialism for divine inspirations—about training and disciplining the children. Laughingly, she asked, "Does this include my husband?"

I replied, "Yes, it does, but it also includes you. Don't you think that both of you have been acting rather like children?" She agreed.

"However," I reassured her, "Jesus said, 'Unless you turn and become like children, you will never enter the kingdom of heaven.' Children, I explained, are receptive to instruction and responsive to DIVINE LOVE. And as to the kingdom, when some of His people asked Jesus where it was, He told them it was within them. This astounded some of His listeners, for they were convinced it was up in the sky someplace."

The mother was very attentive as I continued: "Heaven is a state of consciousness wherein you acknowledge that God is wiser than you, and you realize that if you are to work with the best possible ideas, or concepts, and enjoy the best possible results, you need to be enlightened. You need to be infinitely wise, rather than cunning; you need to have an inflow of unending energy and stamina; you need the help of every element essential to the accomplishment of your objective. You need, in other words, to be divinely LOVED, and to LOVE divinely, for DIVINE LOVE, remember, is the power that attracts to you, all that is good for you, all that helps you fulfill your mission—that is, its positive pole—while at the same time repelling from you all that is not good for you, all that is detrimental to you in any way, all that hinders you in your efforts—that is, its negative pole."

This fine and receptive young wife and mother agreed that what she actually was seeking, was the kingdom of heaven. She wanted, with all her heart, to have a "heavenly" home life and marriage. She wanted her children to behave like "little angels," most of the time, anyway. She wanted her husband to thoroughly appreciate his angelic children, and his capable, competent, and loving wife, so that he would be the fulfillment of all her dreams of what a husband and father should be.

The transformation did not come overnight. It took many weeks of steadfast prayer and effort based upon divine inspirations on her part and faithful counselling support of her efforts and prayers, both in person and by telephone. Whenever she felt low or dubious, she would telephone, and if necessary, come in and talk and pray with us. She would return home reinforced with a spiritual strength and an awareness of God in the midst of her as DIVINE LOVE, in particular, and allness in general.

But the transformation did come. First of all, it was she who was transformed. She began not to feel put upon and sorry for herself. She began to see the good in her sons, no matter what. They were very active boys, alert, energetic, and creative. She became glad that this was so. She praised them for it.

The mother began, too, to see great good in her husband, to appreciate all the things he did which heretofore she had not recognized, or had merely taken for granted—which is a terrible thing to do. After a few weeks they were using the DIVINE LOVE prayer together. Prior to that the husband had never heard of such a thing.

She herself became radiantly healthy, happy, and responsive to the needs of every member of her family; they, in turn, became so in respect to her needs. Freely, she gave of a new kind of LOVE, divine in origin, infinite in scope, and delightful in application. Freely DIVINE LOVE gave to her all the goodness, joy, peace, order, and harmony—complete fulfillment in every phase of her marriage—for which she had yearned. Together, she and her husband loved and trained and disciplined their sons, under divine guidance, who were transformed from unruly, disobedient, quarrelsome boys into wonderfully happy expressions of DIVINE LOVE.

Do Not Judge Others

Ministers, doctors, social workers, and personal counsellors are most successful in helping others if they never indicate surprise or shock at the self-revelations of those who consult them. Their purpose is not to pass judgment, to deplore, or to condemn, but to consider what seem to be the factors in the problem presented, what solutions are acceptable to the patient or counsellee. The counsellor may believe that he has answers that are superior to those that the patient can accept, but his problem is to help the patient find the answers that he can live with most comfortably. And not infrequently what the patient needs is not some prescription or profound advice, not to be either praised for his successes and virtues or condemned for his shortcomings, but to be understood.

A minister who was attending a convention entered a lounge in the hotel where the convention was held. Delighted to see some of his fellow ministers sitting around a table, he was dismayed by the sudden silence that fell upon the group as he approached. One of the younger of the group broke the silence by explaining, "We were just talking about you, when you somewhat startled us by suddenly appearing in the doorway."

"That's interesting," the newcomer remarked. "What did you find interesting to talk about?"

"We were puzzled about why it is that wherever you go, you always attract such a large congregation."

"That has puzzled a good many people. I sometimes wonder about it myself."

"I think I know the answer," the young minister volunteered.

"What do you think it is?" the newcomer invited.

"I think it is not your brilliance, or oratory, or anything like that."

"I don't have much of those qualities."

"It is simply that you LOVE people."

Never underestimate the power of unselfish LOVE. The instructor in a ministerial training school once told his students, referring to a well-known minister: "If you want an example of a man who has made a successful career out of just one idea, I can name you one. No matter what his subject is, it always turns out to be LOVE."

It would be difficult to choose any one subject as the theme for a lifetime career that could equal LOVE.

It has to be genuine.

There are many counterfeits, many pretenders to that throne. Possessiveness is one. So are self-interest, and sentimentality, and domination ("I am only doing this because I LOVE you and want to save you from getting hurt"). The inmate within us senses these shams, and if we live close enough to it, we avoid being deceived by what may even be unconscious or unintended deceptions.

There is a difference between loving and liking, too. A missionary returning to this country from Asia was asked how he felt about the soldiers of a warring country, where he tried to serve young people especially. He seemed lost in thought for a few moments before he spoke. Finally he answered, "I LOVE them, but I do not like them." He loved the sinners, but did not like the things with which they identified themselves.

When We Look With Eyes of Love

There is so much more to all of us than the obvious.

A few times in my life I have gotten a glimpse of the real self of a person. It was only for an anguished moment and only because I looked with eyes of LOVE.

But for an anguished moment I looked with eyes of LOVE and I saw. I cannot say what I saw, but I knew that it was something inexpressibly beautiful. I shall always believe I was looking at being as it really is, and I saw beauty naked.

I believe that is what I would see if I saw the real self of you. But I have to look with eyes of LOVE.

That is why LOVERS go around starry-eyed. They have seen through what is form to what is real, and it has left them dazzled. They can only murmur, "Beautiful."

We look at what they are looking at and wonder how they can see so much in such a plain creature. But it is our vision that is imperfect.

LOVE raises vision to a higher power that eye charts cannot measure.

Your Greatest Power

One of the most important steps in achieving mental and emotional maturity is learning to forgive—to make allowances for and forgive those who we think have wronged us; to forgive ourself for our own mistakes and profit from them; to forgive life for the cruel and wearisome pummeling of blows that are usually self-inflicted.

Suppose that ten years ago your best friend John wronged you in some way. And suppose that, at the time John dealt with you unjustly, you got a big stick and started beating yourself over the head with it. To make matters worse, suppose that ever since that sorry day ten years ago, you have carried that big stick around with you everywhere you went, so that in case you should happen to recall what John did to you, you could start beating yourself over the head again. Wouldn't that be ridiculous? But unforgiveness is just as foolish as that. Your animosity and unforgiveness will not hurt John, or cause him to repent, but they will be very hard on you, and a mature person does not willfully do things that are harmful to himself. If you are holding any resentment or unforgiveness toward anyone in your world, you are (figuratively speaking) beating yourself over the head. You are hurting yourself, upsetting your body chemistry, undermining your health, destroying your happiness and peace of mind, and closing a channel of your being to the action of God. It isn't mature or sensible.

Solomon said, "With all thy getting get understanding." We can learn a great deal from those who wrong us. Why should we condemn a person who has helped us achieve greater wisdom and understanding? Our enemies often come bearing rich gifts.

Forgiveness, of course, is not something that is to be extended only to others. We must also learn to forgive ourself. In Bunyan's *Pilgrim's Progress*, poor Pilgrim struggled through his long journey carrying strapped to his back a very heavy burden of guilt. Nearly everyone in the world is carrying a similar burden, not strapped on his back, but festering like a painful sore deep within the mind and heart. Such a person wakes up in the middle of the night when he should be sleeping, and he tosses and turns in torment because he cannot forgive himself for mistakes he has made in the past, for hurts he has inflicted on loved ones, or for times when he has failed to live up to his own ideals and standards of behaviour.

Here again is the foolishness of the big stick. Suppose that ten years ago, you wronged John. You did something unforgivable and hurt him badly. You then got a big stick, and ever since then, whenever you think of what you did to John, you pick up the stick and beat yourself over the head with it. The memory of the past mistakes is not something to be carried as a burden, but something to be dealt with. We are supposed to do something about these memories, and the thing that Jesus told us to do was to find forgiveness through atonement and repentance.

I love the definition of repentance that a Sunday-school teacher received from one of her children: "To repent is to be sorry enough to quit." And so it is in forgiving ourself for the mistakes of the past. The important thing is that we have reached the state of mind wherein we say, "I will never make the same mistakes again. I'm sorry it happened, and I'll never let it happen again." If possible, we should make amends to those we have wronged: but the main thing is to forgive ourself and to accept the forgiveness of God. God always understands. As the Psalmist said, "He knoweth our frame."

The Work of Love and Intelligence

I believe that the world is the work of a Divine LOVE and a Divine Intelligence, which for want of a better word I call God.

God may be more than LOVE—but He cannot be less. Anything less is unthinkable. If the world is not the work of LOVE, it is not the work of anything; it is blind chance stumbling over blind chaos.

Even I put LOVE into my world as far as I am able to—imperfectly because I do not yet know how to love more—but God is Perfect LOVE.

Therefore, the world must be the perfect work of Perfect LOVE. It may be more—but it cannot be less.

The world must be the work of Perfect Intelligence, too (for God—by the only definition worthy of the name—must be Perfect Intelligence as well as Perfect LOVE).

The world, then, is not put together in a bungling fashion, but is shaped as Perfect Intelligence would shape a world it made. The Potter did not make some of his pots with flaws!

We look at the world and at a glance we see much that does not look perfect. The world has sickness and pain in it. The world has loneliness and growing old in it. The world has loss and tears in it. The world has wounds and death in it. In this world we do not always get what we want and we do not always want what we get.

If it is a good world, then the pain must be there for a purpose—because it leads to good—a greater good than we would come to without it. The pain must be there because it is necessary—and will be there only as long as it is necessary.

To believe that the world and life and you are the good work of a good God, you have to believe two things to be true.

One. You are immortal.

Two. Something in you—call it what you may—draws your own life to you.

The Lesser Good

As human beings we conceive of and are aware of only a small part of that which is great. At one time all humanity thought the world was flat; this conception did not make the earth flat. It was a misconception, and it was only four hundred and seventy-five years ago. We have a greater misconception about ourselves and our relationship to God.

We turn to God to find us a parking place, to take care of our finances, to get Johnny home on time. We are told not a sparrow falls to the ground without God's knowledge, but God does not stop here, this is just part of God. We are to trust God every moment with all that concerns us. Let's know that God's care of us in the little things is just to remind us how great is the power that takes care of us always. The power within you is God, and with it all things are possible. It is a power that can heal the sick, raise the dead, and change the path of man and bring forth a new world. Yet we only take the scraps from the table of God.

We have found and proven the power of the mind; we have built a fantastic world; we know that all that is in our world is brought forth by the mind, but we do not dream of what the Spirit can do. We have stopped short of our goal. We know the mind and the things that come forth from mind without knowing the soul and Spirit in which the mind rests. We do not have the fullness of life but only a small portion.

There is so much more to life than the share we are taking. We say we have demonstrated truth, but we have not demonstrated all the truth. In our struggle for life we have taken only a small portion of what is ours by divine right. We tremble, and this trembling takes hold of the mighty. The Scripture reminds us, "Let not your hearts faint, fear not, and do not tremble, neither be ye terrified. . . . for the Lord, your God, is He that goeth with you." (Deut. 20: 3, 4) There is a divine and perfect plan of life and our soul knows and we tremble.

Gibran, the poet from Lebanon, in his book, *The Prophet,* speaks of the shepherd boy who stands before the King, whose hand is to be laid upon him in honour. He says, "Yet is not the shepherd boy more aware of his own trembling, than he is of the mark of the King?" This is the way it is with us. We are more aware of our trembling than we are of the fact that each experience lifts us into the Presence of our God. We do not understand that all the little experiences of life that happen and perhaps aggravate us are a part of an infinite plan and all for our advancement. We are not aware that the experiences of life work a great advantage in us. Fear is to call forth courage and faith. That use of good is the only wealth; if you give freely of the gift which is yours, you can only give to yourself.

Let Love Happen

Would you like to have people think of you as a loving person? Would you like to know how to harness the alleged miracle-working power of Love? Would you like to know what Love is? Would you like to be loved?

> Then — Stop trying to be loving.
> Stop seeking to harness the power of Love.
> Stop trying to define Love.
> Stop seeking to be loved.

Instead—Let there be only one Love in your life. God.

Rendezvous with Him in silent meditation. Bask in the Love-Light of His presence. Let that Light shine through the lens of your "I" to impart understanding. Passionately seek His Will and His Wisdom.

Do not depend on people or things for fulfillment, security, or Love—depend only on God. Become God-enfused, God-enthused, God-intoxicated, God-dependent.

> And then magically, effortlessly Love happens.
> You are a loving person: the miracle
> working power of Love moves through you,
> you are Love, and you are loved.

Command Performance

The "Good Book" says,
"You shall LOVE your neighbour as yourself,"
So—I LOVE me . . . all of me,
I LOVE the height and depth, the length and breadth of me,
The humanity, divinity, infinity of me,
 I LOVE the unfettered, unlimited, boundless me,
For I am the image of God, the light of the world,
And the kingdom of God is within me.

AND

I LOVE you . . . all of you.
I LOVE the height and depth, the length and breadth of you,
The humanity, divinity, infinity of you.
I LOVE the unfettered, unlimited, boundless you,
For you are the image of God, the light of the world,
And the kingdom of God is within you.

Let My People Go!

According to the story in the book of Genesis, God's first creation was Light. Then He proceeded to bring into manifestation all the "Good" necessary for His last creation, Man, who was made in His image and after His own likeness. His child, His offspring, Man, then was introduced into a world all prepared for him. Light is symbolic of wisdom and intelligence, the first needful requisite of Man, to properly understand his relationship with God, the mystery of his creation, and to utilize with good judgment the lavish provisions of his creator.

Perhaps Man did not devote the time nor energy necessary to know himself, and the story unfolds with these lofty creations of God in slavery and bondage to the ungodly. In Egypt—which is symbolic of a state of mind of darkness and ignorance, an unillumined consciousness, they dwelt in the shackles of despair and distress. They must have conditioned themselves so thoroughly to this state of existence that they accepted it as their way of life. Yet, deep within them must have lingered that spark of yearning for something better which had been their experience in the distant past. For Man was created to dwell in the Light, to be wise with the wisdom of God expressing through him.

It is no wonder then that Moses was inspired to take action in the release of his brothers in bondage. From the same source of wisdom which in the work of creation pronounced the words "Let it be!" now emanated the instructions to be delivered to the Pharaoh "LET MY PEOPLE GO!" Simply but conclusively conveying—let my people be removed from the darkness of ignorance, misery, lack, idolatrous beliefs, tribulation, and distress. Let them know themselves to be my children of Light.

For further elucidation a code for living was handed to Moses. The first article of that code demanded recognition of one God, the mighty I AM, and was particularly emphatic that there must be no belief in any other God: That there was, and is no other Omnipotent One. There is but ONE PRESENCE and ONE POWER—it is GOD—it is GOOD—it is OMNIPOTENT. The understanding and acceptance of this Truth keeps us in the Light.

It is this All Wise, All Powerful, All Loving, All Good Presence which Jesus Christ acknowledged with every iota of His Being. In this Light, and with this Power for GOOD, He was able to let good express through Him in His words and works. He healed the sick, raised the dead, gave sight to the blind, provided abundance when lack was apparent, indicating clearly and at all times that He was working with God Power. He was doing exactly what His Father wanted Him to do, since it was the Father within Him doing the works.

More necessary than ever is the need today for believers in God, to stand tall and express as God wants them to. That there is but ONE PRESENCE—GOD and He is GOOD: There is not another Power called evil, nor another "OMNIPOTENT" called Satan whom we are called upon to fight. The idea of fighting someone or something, is acknowledging it as a formidable reality, a something that could be instrumental in producing adverse effects in our lives: a something to which we must give our attention.

The first commandment declares that all our attention must be directed to the Truth of one GOD. There must be no room in our minds for beliefs to the contrary: If we are only partially convinced, and *believe* in another power called evil (or by any other name) we set up another "GOD," and we may be influencing others to pay undue attention to this "GOD": to attribute some of the happenings in their life to this non-existent "POWER."

Try and stretch your imagination, and envision the sublimity that this world would experience if every day people of all religions could sincerely decree this Truth "There is but ONE PRESENCE IN THIS UNIVERSE, IT IS GOD (or Allah, Jehovah, Brahman, or whatever name identifies the Omnipresent One) IT IS GOOD, IT IS ALL POWERFUL": If only this could be the Universal creed, accepted by all believers in God (in Good). There would be no need for some persons to seek devious methods to combat "evil." Those who now make a living by catering to people who

acknowledge evil as a power, would have to change their vocations. The "appearance" of evil may become something to
reckon with, if the mind makes it so. It is nothing when it
remains no thing: Where does the darkness go when the Light
is introduced? Light is a reality, it is forever permanent. Ignorance can be transformed, and it disappears with the illumination
that is the Truth; The Wisdom of the Infinite.

If we are propounding the idea of the existence of two
Powers, God and the devil, think on it, we could be aiding the
workers of iniquity. We could be subsidizing their earnings, and
helping to foster their existence: We can hardly condemn them,
when through our very teachings they appoint themselves to
deal with a "Power" that we may have helped to create. We
could be a party to keeping God's people in darkness. There is
a contribution we all should be willing to make. Plato one of
the illumined souls who lived about 400 years before the birth
of Jesus Christ philosophized "that Man has an individual and
social responsibility when he has seen something of the Light,
he has to assist others to also see that Light."

Right thinking precipitates right expressions and right action.
These contribute to the elimination of adverse conditions in our
lives. "Thou shalt have no other gods before me"—the I AM—the
FATHER—GOD. Thou shalt LOVE (pay attention) to this GOD—with
every iota of your Being, leaving no avenue of thought for the
recognition of "something else as a reality." Be assured that this
concept or any other thought, word, or deed, calculated to
bring mankind into closer relationship with GOD, with LOVE,
helps to eradicate the darkness or sin of wrong thinking, and is
a torch lit for the freedom of God's people.

Let my people go! Let them be immersed in the Light of
Truth. Let them know that they are my children, blessed with
my breath of life, not as a result of an outward ceremony, or
ritual. I their God AM ONE, and there is none other. Let them
be freed from thoughts of hate, beliefs in fear, greed, doubts,
envy, and false concepts, which they will unwittingly make
their "gods." Let them know I AM LOVE, and that I need them
to express my good, and to bask in the Light of my WISDOM AND

INTELLIGENCE. Speak these words of Truth fearlessly. Speak them boldly. They will be accepted if they are repeated, and repeated and repeated—and proven when felt.

THERE IS ONLY ONE GOD—THE GOOD. THE ALL-WISE. THE ALL-POWERFUL. THE ALL-LOVING. AND MY SPIRIT AND PRESENCE IS IN-DIVIDUALIZED IN ALL MY CHILDREN: THIS IS THE FREEING TRUTH— that will LET MY PEOPLE GO!

Faith in Your Dream

It may well be that our lack of individual and world faith is indeed merely lack of a need big enough. This thought comes to me again and again when I go over my case histories of instantaneous healings by prayer. When the need is big enough, meaning when we care enough, it seems to generate faith in tremendous proportions to what it is at any other time. For a world example, we remember Dunkirk. Hitler, we recall, had announced that he had bottled up the British Army, and would annihilate it. The King of England called for a day of prayer. The whole Christian world joined the British in going into their churches, and down on their knees to pray for deliverance. And deliverance came. It was my privilege to work with a small prayer group at that time, and to this hour I can feel the wave of hope that came in time after time. It was as though the whole world was holding its breath while the Holy Comforter, the law of the Lord, took things in hand.

When it is a life or death matter, our faith rises to meet the need. This brings our circle full again, we are back to where we started in the previous article. LOVE is the law of life. If we LOVE enough we will have faith.

This gives us a rule of life: Acts of LOVE develop faith.
If ye have faith, as a grain of mustard seed, ye shall say unto this mountain. Remove hence to yonder place, and it shall remove, and nothing shall be impossible unto you. (Matt. 17:20, A.V.)

But we need to understand this fact, for the reason is subtle. We long have been conditioned to the idea of "be good, or God will not LOVE you." The idea is implanted in the child's mind at an early age—"be good or Santa Claus will not bring you anything"—and is continued all through our growing lives. Reward for good behaviour and punishment for misbehaviour have become a part of our heart by the time we are grown. We consciously and unconsciously carry this belief over into our thoughts about and our relationship with God. The hidden belief that God does not LOVE me because I am bad, has sent many people into mental illness, as every psychiatrist, psychologist, and religious counsellor knows. Even our fundamentalist ministers are learning it. There is a growing literature about the fact that many good Christians, including ministers, become mentally ill over this point of religion. That is the extreme side of it. Long before we reach that point of desperation, we will have lost faith in our dream and in most of our daily hopes and works.

We must look farther:

Man is born needing: status with God, status with his fellow-men, and status with himself. His faith in all life, in his abilities, in the work he is trying to do can be accurately measured by what he believes is his standing with God, neighbour, and what he secretly thinks about himself as a living soul. In his monumental book, *Men Who Have Walked with God*, Sheldon Cheney opens his preface with the words:

"In the final analysis there is only one subject of permanent interest, the soul."

It is a truth. In his quiet, sane, and unhurried moments, every man knows from a wisdom from within that earth-life is but a breadth of time, and that the soul's highest duty is to try to learn to work with God. And our greatest joy and material success alike come from learning the spiritual laws and how to work consciously with them, and so with God. When we come to that, there are no fears left for us on this earth. There can be no real faith, no growth, so long as we feel we are not LOVED by God. We should go to bed every night of our life feeling, knowing, "God LOVES me, no matter what I do." Any other feeling is damaging to our daily faith and soul growth.

There just is no way to separate LOVE and faith.

The Prospering Power of Love

A housewife had worried for many months over her husband's illness. The more she tried to help him recover, the more he seemed to cling to his illness, and the more confined they both were. One day she learned of the healing power of release, and began to declare for her husband. "I release you now to your highest good. I love you, and I release you to complete freedom and complete health in whatever way best. I am free, and you are free."

When this woman had previously tried to help her husband by using various healing affirmations, he had seemed subconsciously to resist her attempts to will him to health. After she began to release him to find health in his own way, ceasing any mental effort in his direction, and began to lead a more normal life herself, her husband's health rapidly improved. Some of his former ailments disappeared completely. He experienced the healing power of LOVE, as it worked through release.

Most human-relations problems would melt away, if people would practice the healing power of release, instead of trying to make people over in a certain image, or trying to force them to do things in a certain way.

Nowhere is there more need for the expression of LOVE as release than between husbands and wives, between parents and children. We often try to bend others to our will, calling it LOVE when it is really selfish possessiveness that binds instead of frees. Then we wonder why others resist instead of accepting our "help."

Gibran described the loving attitude of release in marriage: "LOVE one another, but make not a bond of LOVE . . . let there be spaces in your togetherness. . . . Sing and dance together and be joyous, but let each one of you be alone . . . stand together yet not too near together."

A world-renowned sociologist has conducted research studies at Harvard University on the power of LOVE. Under his direction, a staff of scientists studied the subject of LOVE. Their findings were that LOVE, like other good things, can be produced deliberately by human beings. They stated that there is no reason why we cannot learn to generate LOVE as we do other natural forces.

Thus there is no reason for you to feel disillusioned or disappointed if LOVE has seemingly let you down or passed you by. Those who bitterly declare that their lives are without LOVE are mistakenly looking to someone or something outside themselves for LOVE. Begin realizing now that LOVE is first within you, and can be released through your thoughts, feelings, words, and actions. As you begin developing LOVE from within outward, you are truly proving your method to be spiritual, scientific, and satisfying. You become master of your world, and free from hurt, fear, disappointment, and disillusionment.

LOVE will begin to radiate outwardly into every part of your world, to attract to you the right people, situations, and conditions that will add to your success and happiness. You will soon realize that instead of your being at the mercy of the world, the world responds to your own thoughts and feelings, and that when your own thoughts and feelings generate LOVE, the world about you will happily respond in a most wonderful way. This is the success power of LOVE.

Many people are discovering this power in all departments of life.

From the New Testament

But I say unto you, love your enemies, bless them that curse you, do good to them that hate you, and pray for them which despitefully use you, and persecute you.

That ye may be the children of your Father which is in heaven, for He maketh the sun to rise on the evil and on the good, and sendeth rain on the just, and the unjust. (Matt. 5:44)

For if ye love them which love you, what thanks have ye? do not even the publicans the same? (Matt. 5:46)

Honour thy father and thy mother, and thou shalt love thy neighbour as thyself. (Matt. 19:19)

Jesus said unto them, "Thou shalt love the Lord thy God with all thy heart, and with all thy soul, and with all thy mind."

This is the first and great commandment.

And the second is like unto it, "Thou shalt love thy neighbour as thyself."

On these two commandments hang all the laws and the prophets. (Matt. 22:37-40)

But I say unto you which hear, Love your enemies, do good to them which hate you.

For if ye love them which love you, what thank have ye? for sinners also do even the same. (St. Luke 6:27-32)

This is my commandment, That ye love one another as I have loved you.

Greater love hath no man than this, that a man lay down his life for his friends. (John 15:12-13)

And we know that all things work together for good to them

that love God, to them who are called according to his purpose. (Romans 8:28)

Who shall separate us from the love of Christ? shall tribulation or distress, or persecution, or famine, or nakedness, or peril, or sword?

For I am persuaded that neither death, nor life, nor angels, nor principalities, nor powers, nor things present, nor things to come.

Nor height, nor depth, nor any other creature, shall be able to separate us from the love of God, which is in Christ Jesus our Lord. (Romans 8:35-39)

Owe no man anything, but to love one another, for he that loveth another hath fulfilled the law.

For this, Thou shalt not commit adultery, Thou shalt not kill, Thou shalt not steal, Thou shalt not bear false witness, Thou shalt not covet, and if there be any other commandment, it is briefly comprehended in this saying, namely, Thou shalt love thy neighbour as thyself.

Love worketh no ill to his neighbour, therefore love is the fulfilling of the law. (Romans 13:8-15)

But as it is written, Eye hath not seen, nor ear heard, neither have entered into the heart of man, the things which God hath prepared for them that love him. (1 Cor. 2:9)

Knowledge puffeth up, but love edifieth.

And if any man think that he knoweth anything, he knoweth nothing, yet as he ought to know.

But if any man love God, the same is known to him. (1 Cor. 8:1-3)

Though I speak with the tongues of men and of angels, and have not love, I am become as sounding brass, or a tinkling cymbal.

And though I have the gift of prophecy, and understand

all mysteries, and all knowledge, and though I have all faith, so that I could remove mountains, and have not love, I am nothing.

And though I bestow all my goods to feed the poor, and though I give my body to be burned, and have not love, it profiteth nothing.

Love suffereth long and is kind; love envieth not; love vaunteth not itself, is not puffed up.

Doth not behave itself unseemly, seeketh not her own, is not easily provoked, thinketh no evil.

Rejoiceth not in iniquity, but rejoiceth in the truth.

Beareth all things, believeth all things, hopeth all things, endureth all things.

Love never faileth; but whether there be prophecies they shall fail; whether there be tongues, they shall cease, whether there be knowledge it shall vanish away.

For we know in part, and we prophesy in part.

But when that which is perfect is come, then that which is in part shall be done away.

When I was a child, I spoke as a child, I understood as a child, I thought as a child, but when I became a man, I put away childish things.

For now we see through a glass darkly; but then face to face: now I know in part, but then shall I know even as also I am known.

And now abideth faith, hope, love, these three; but the greatest of these is love. (1 Cor. 13:1-13)

For in Jesus Christ neither circumcision availeth anything, nor uncircumcision; but faith which worketh by love. (Gal. 5:6)

But let us, who are of the day be sober, putting on the breastplate of faith and love, and for an helmet the hope of salvation. (1 Thess. 5:8)

For God is not unrighteous to forget your work and labour

of love, which ye have showed toward His name, in that ye have ministered to the saints and do minister. (Heb. 6:10)

Let brotherly love continue. (Heb. 13:1)

Honour all men. Love the brotherhood. Love God. Honour the King. (1 Pet. 2:17)

Ye are of God, little children, and have overcome them: because greater is He that is in you, than He that is in the world.

Beloved let us love one another: for love is of God: and everyone that loveth is born of God, and knoweth God.

He that loveth not knoweth not God: for God is love.

No man hath seen God at anytime. If we love one another, God dwelleth in us, and his love is perfected in us.

Hereby know we that we dwell in Him, and He in us because he hath given us of His spirit. (1 John 4:4-13)

And we have known and believed the love that God hath to us. God is love: and he that dwelleth in love dwelleth in God, and God in Him.

Herein is our love made perfect that we may have boldness in the day of judgment; because as He is, so are we in this world.

There is no fear in love, but perfect love casteth out all fear: because fear hath torment. He that feareth, is not made perfect in love.

We love him because He first loved us.

If a man say, I love God and hateth his brother, he is a liar, for he that loveth not his brother, whom he hath seen, how can he love God whom he hath not seen?

And this commandment have we from Him. That he who loveth God, love his brother also. (1 John 4:16-21)

What Is Good About Good Friday?

Greater Love Hath No Man

Every year Christians all over the world commemorate the death of Jesus, on a cross at Calvary, nearly two thousand years ago. It marks an event that was shocking in its cruelty, terrifying in its sadism and savagery. Yet, somehow, it has pleased the world to call the day Good Friday.

When we look back at historical events, we find that on the days of tragic occurrences, a descriptive adjective has generally been used to identify that day. For example: a Monday may be called "black" Monday, when people recall a tragic event on that day: a Tuesday may be designated as "bloody" Tuesday, because of some grim event that transpired on that day. Generally there is an appropriate and befitting adjective to connect the day to the occurrence.

But we are considering a day on which a man went about doing good, healing the sick, giving sight to the blind, teaching, blessing, loving; a man who, in short, was the most perfect manifestation of God in human form; a man who was ignominiously treated and put to death in a manner that, even in those days, was inflicted only on the worst type of criminals. This day is known by the world as Good Friday.

Would you say that this is mildly paradoxical?

Let us, then, try to arrive at the origin of the name Good Friday. Research tells us that Good Friday was the English name for the Friday before Easter, which was considered the anniversary of the Crucifixion. The term is probably a corruption of "God's Friday," and it was on this day that services were held to mark the day when mourning and rigorous fasting were observed. All of this was considered to be Godlike—thus the name "God's Friday."

On Good Friday in Spain before the 7th century, churches

were closed as a sign of mourning. Later, in Rome, altars and priests were draped in black, and sad and mournful services were conducted.

When we think of it today as Good Friday, we automatically concede it to be God's Friday, since God and good are synonymous. And surely it is God's Friday, because on this day, we recall vividly the world's greatest demonstration of Love and of the powers of God as expressed through man. It was a day when the spiritual powers with which God endowed man were revealed at the peak of perfection.

Let us pause for a moment to consider what strength and will it took for Jesus to allow Himself to be humiliated and abused—to be condemned by the Sanhedrin and brought before Pilate, to be spat upon, to be cursed, to be crowned with thorns, and to be nailed to a wooden cross like a common malefactor. What strength! What will!

He uttered the words "Peace! Be still!" and the raging seas ceased their tumultuous vehemence. He walked through an angry, threatening mob, yet no man lifted a finger to harm Him. He rebuked devils, commanded demons. He called the dead back to life!

Was not every iota of this faith and understanding necessary to visualize what was at the end of this agonizing experience? It must have taken greater power than he had ever before used in order to restrain Himself throughout the ordeal, in order to get across to humanity the message of His mission—the way He demonstrated was the "way and the truth, and the life."

What message of forgiving Love did He demonstrate when He prayed that prayer on the cross? Greater Love has no man than this! It was the true, unadulterated Love of God expressed through man for all men.

And so the question is answered for us. What is good about Good Friday? It is Good Friday because God's Love was expressed through man in its most magnificent and radiantly embracing form—at its Godliest. With that thought let us resolve to observe the two great laws—that of loving God, and loving our fellowmen. Let us cleanse ourselves of all resentments and unforgiving thoughts to which we may be clinging, and allow the Christ Love to fill our hearts and minds.

Let us think of faith as most profound—at its extreme—at its height. Faith as accepting the will and the guidance of God in the understanding that, notwithstanding appearances to the contrary, only good can and will come into our life.

Let us think of the renunciation that preceded the crucifixion, the complete obliteration of doubts, fears, and all the negative attitudes. Let us think of the zeal that brought Jesus' awareness of oneness with God the Father, of the continual exercise of good judgment, and of the imagination which stood sentry with faith.

And finally let us think of life and its indestructibility, and know that Jesus came to give us the gospel of life not death. Let us realise that we are blessed with the selfsame spiritual powers with which Jesus was blessed, and let us try to perfect them as He did. He said, "He who believes in me, will also do the works that I do! And greater works than these will he do, because I go to my Father."

So on Good Friday there is no need to be morbid, to be depressed, grief stricken, or mournful. It is a good day, for it is God's day. Let us remember that in the last grand climax, when the curtain seemed to fall on the act, Jesus was in fact telling the world—loud and clear and with greater emphasis than words could ever express—that life is eternal, that the way He shows us is the "way and the truth, and the life." He was also telling us that all men have access to oneness with the Christ by the acceptance of Jesus' words, His teaching, and His example.

This is why we can think of Good Friday *as good!*

The Contemplation of Christ

LOVE—His LOVE for humanity—was the power that enabled Jesus to heal; that and their response to His LOVE.

LOVE is the power that heals men today. Men are seldom successful in throwing off by a process of reasoning the burdens of sin and sickness that weigh down the mind and body. The power that heals is more than one of intellectual perception. We may know all the rules of a game, and still not be able to play it well. We may know all the rules of right thinking, and still be unable to apply our knowledge practically for bodily and mental health. We must feel the truth of what we mentally perceive. "As he (man) thinketh in his heart, so is he." (A.V) In his heart, not in his mind.

The doctrine of Jesus Christ is a heart doctrine.

This element of Christianity perplexes many students who approach Christianity from the letter rather than from the spirit of Christ's teachings. Paul, perceiving this in his time, said to the Romans, "But now we have been discharged from the law, having died to that wherein we were held; so that we serve in newness of the spirit, and not in oldness of the letter," and again, "The letter killeth, but the spirit giveth life."

A certain modern healer is very successful in helping those who appeal to her. A younger friend and student was much interested in her success, and very curious concerning her method.

He tried to analyze her practices, and to find their secret. He learned that she ordinarily devoted about twenty minutes to an interview, that she invariably sat in the same room, in the same chair, that her patient sat opposite her, that sometimes she spoke an audible prayer, but more frequently prayed silently.

His healer friend seemed willing to answer his questions, but also seemed a little troubled, almost hurt, by them.

"Do you always sit in the same chair, in the same room?"

"Yes."

"Do you think there is more power present there than elsewhere?"

"No, of course not," she answered patiently. "Doing my work there is more convenient than elsewhere. It is quiet, and I am accustomed to the surroundings and like them."

"Do you exert a force of will to heal your patients, or do you use the power of suggestion on them?"

"Neither—not consciously at any rate!"

"Then what do you think gets the results?"

She seemed almost embarrassed for the first time in the conversation. She flushed just a little. "I'm afraid you will be disappointed," she answered. "It seems too simple to amount to much. I just LOVE them into getting well."

She was apologetic for the simplicity of her answer. Truly that answer might not be accepted as having great scientific weight, for somehow science has not yet gotten around to such study of the miraculous powers that are wrapped up in the simple guise of compassionate LOVE. Yet quite possibly this simple woman of great heart was, in her answer, nearer to the real secret of Christ's power than are all the learned psychologists who have analyzed His methods and His power.

God Is My Father

One of the most delightful and productive mind-stretching experiences comes when we change our ancestry from mere human to Divine. Jesus, the greatest mind-stretcher of all time, gave us the key to this sweeping ancestry change in these words: "Call no man your father . . . for you have one Father, who is in heaven." He also urged that all with the courage and faith to follow Him pray to "Our Father who art in heaven."

Take this revelation of truth into your mind, entertain it, give it operating room, think it through. Since God is your Father you are a son of the Infinite, offspring of the Almighty, heir to the riches of the Most High. Since God is also the Father of the rest of humanity, all men—regardless of race, color, religion, politics—are members of the same divine family, and it is your privilege and blessing to regard them in this way.

As you continue to meditate on the truth of being and to contemplate its potential, you will discover some far-reaching changes in the operation of your mind. Your attitudes toward God, toward yourself, toward your neighbour, toward your family will improve. Smallness of thought, prejudice, selfishness, racial or religious bias will have less and less appeal to you. It will dawn on you that you are gradually becoming a new creature, daily going through the process that has been aptly termed the "new truth." The horizons of your mind will move out and out, and you will be able to include more of humanity, more of the whole universe in your acceptance.

Following are some Mind Stretchers in words to help you change your ancestry, or to put it more accurately, to accept your ancestry as it has always been in truth.

God is my Father. I am a son of the Infinite, offspring of the Almighty, heir to the riches of the Most High.

God is my Father. I am a son of the Infinite, and I am beginning to feel, think, speak, and act like one.

God is my Father. I am a son of the Infinite, and I pray like one. Use this before every prayer, especially before the Lord's Prayer, and you will find the depth, power, and effectiveness of your prayer expanding miraculously.

God is my Father. I am a son of the Infinite, and I rejoice in a wonderful, dynamic, creative, healthy relationship with my heavenly Father.

God is my Father. I am a son of the Infinite. I give like one. I receive like one. I conduct my business like one. I pay my bills like one. I am beginning to live like one, and I like it.

God is the Father of my neighbour. He is a son of the Infinite. I treat him like one. I LOVE my neighbour as myself.

God is the Father of the universe, and I am at home in it.

"I Am" Discourses

By the Ascended Master Saint Germain

Every breath you breathe is *God in Action in You.* Your ability to express or read forth thought and feeling is GOD acting in you. You, having free will, it is entirely up to you to qualify the energy sent forth in your thought and feeling, and determine how it shall act for you.

111

The admonition has been before humanity through many centuries: "Ye cannot serve two masters." Why is this so? First: because there is only ONE INTELLIGENCE, ONE PRESENCE, ONE POWER that can act, and that is the Presence of God acting in you. When you turn to the outer manifestation, and give all kinds of expressions and appearances power, you are attempting to serve a false, usurping master, because the outer expression can only find an appearance through the use of God's Mighty Energy.

111

The outer experience of Life is but a constant changing, passing picture that the outer mind has created in its pretense (imagination) of being the Real Actor. This is the attention so constantly fixed upon the outer, which alone contains imperfection, that the Children of God have forgotten their own Divinity and must come back to It again.

God is the Giver, the Receiver, and the Gift, and is the Sole Owner of all the Intelligence, Substance, Energy, and Opulence there is in the Universe.

If the Children of God would learn to give for the joy of giving, whether it be Love, money, service, or whatever, they would open the door to such vast opulence that it would be impossible to want for a single thing in the outer expression. . . If in every act of the personality God were given full credit, transformations unbelievable could not help taking place in the one thus giving full credit and power where it belongs.

111

It was never intended by the Great All-Wise, All-Loving Father that any of His children should want for a single thing; but because they allow their attention to become fixed on the outer appearance, which is like the changing sands of the desert, they have knowingly or unknowingly cut themselves off to a large degree from that Great Opulence and Intelligence. This Great Opulence is their birthright which everyone can have who will again turn to the "I AM" the Active Principle of God, forever within himself, as the Only Source of Active Life, Intelligence, and Opulence.

111

Again I must remind you that this Limitless Mighty Power of God cannot intrude Its wondrous Powers into your outer use except by your invitation. There is only one kind of invitation that can reach it and loose it, and that is your *feeling* of deep devotion and Love. . . . The soul who is strong enough to clothe itself in its Armour of Divine Love and go forward will find no obstruction, for there is naught between your present consciousness and this Mighty Transcendent Inner Sphere to obstruct the approach of Divine Love.

111

The angry, condemning person who sends out destructive thought, feeling, or speech to another who is poised in his own God power, receives back to himself the quality with which he charged this power, while the poised person receives the energy which serves him, and which he automatically requalifies by his own poise. Thus the creator of discord, through anger and condemnation, is consciously destroying himself, his world of activity, and his affairs.

✦✦✦

God being all Love must have Infinite Patience, and no matter how many mistakes one may have made, he can always once again "Arise and go unto the Father." Such is the Love and Freedom within which God's children are privileged to act.

There is only one Mighty, invincible, evolving process and that is through the power of consciously generating Divine Love. Love being the Hub of all Life, the more we enter in and use It consciously, the more easily and quickly we release this Mighty Power of God, which is always standing as a damned-up force waiting to find an opening in our own consciousness by which it can project Itself.

✦✦✦

Hold the reins of power forever within yourself. People are afraid of just embracing the Great God Power and letting It operate. What is there to fear in God? Its operation is Pure and Perfect, and if you do not reach out to embrace the Great Pure God Power how can you expect to use It and have Perfection?

✦✦✦

The simple key to Perfect Happiness and its inherent sustaining power is Self Control and Self Correction. This is easy to accomplish when one has learned he is the "I AM" Presence and Intelligence, controlling and commanding all things.

Surrounding each individual is a thought-world created by him or her. Within this thought-world is the seed, the "Divine Presence," the "I AM" which is the only acting Presence there is in the Universe, and which directs all energy. This energy can be intensified beyond any limit through the conscious activity of the individual.

The time has arrived when all must understand that thought and feeling are the only and Mightiest Creative Power in Life or in the Universe. Thus the only way to the definite use of the full power of one's thought and feeling, which is *God in Action*, is through Self Control—Self Correction, by which one may quickly reach the attainment; the understanding whereby he may direct and use this Creative Thought-Power without any limit whatsoever.

111

Everyone who manifests in the physical form today has made plenty of mistakes—some time, somewhere—so let no one take the attitude "I AM more holy than thou," but each one's first attitude should be to call on the Law of Forgiveness and if he be feeling or sending criticism, condemnation, or hate to another of God's children, a brother or sister, he can never have enlightenment or success until he calls on the Law of Forgiveness. Further than this, he must say to that person about whom he was feeling disturbed in any way—silently, "I send to you the fullness of the outer activities." For an individual to hold an attitude of revenge for any seeming wrong, imaginary or otherwise, can only bring upon himself incapacity of mind and body. The old yet wondrous statement brought down to us through the ages—"Unless you are willing to forgive, how can you be forgiven," is one of the Mightiest Laws for use in human experience. Oh, that individuals and many students could only see how they hold to themselves the things they do not want by allowing the mind to revolve upon the discordant things which have passed and cannot be helped through the outer senses.

111

So after all, the one who holds vicious thoughts about another is in reality but destroying himself, his business, and his affairs. There is no possible way of averting it except for the individual to awaken and consciously reverse the currents.

↑↑↑

There is perhaps no single element responsible for so many diseased conditions of body and mind as the feeling of hate sent to another individual. There is no telling how this will react upon the mind and body of the sender. In one, it will produce one effect; in another, still a different effect. Let it be here understood that resentment is but another form of hate, only of a milder degree.

↑↑↑

Mankind has not previously understood that Divine Love is a Power, a Presence, an Intelligence, a Light that can be fanned into a Boundless Flame or Fire, and it is within the conscious intelligence of every individual, especially students of the Light, to so create and generate this "Presence of Love" that It becomes an Invincible, Exhaustless, Peace-commanding "Presence" wherever the conscious individual desires to direct It. . . . Love is the First Principle of Life and may be generated to any degree or without any limit whatsoever for Infinite use.

↑↑↑

There is not a moment in the day that we do not visualize something, because the power of vision is acting all the time. Keep all out of the mind except the pictures you want, for that is all with which you are concerned. Do not let the attention become focused on the seeming emptiness.

↑↑↑

Whatever the conscious attention is fixed firmly upon, that quality is impelled into the experience of the individual. Whatever an individual sees with deep feeling within another individual, he frees into his own experience. This is the indisputable proof of why the only desirable feeling to be sent out from any individual is the Presence of Divine Love, and I mean by that Pure Unselfish Love.

�⁊⁊

An awakened individual never uses a destructive force.

⁊⁊⁊

I found that shortly, I was entirely unaware of time or place; and that each day, as I entered more fully into this expansion of consciousness, I found that all things of my desire were right within my individual, governing power; and with it came the consciousness that "Divine Love was the Mighty Cohesive Power, holding all things together and in place—that this Divine Love within me of which I had begun to learn, made me an Invincible Magnet for everything upon which my desire rested."

⁊⁊⁊

(Jesus speaks) The student should constantly look within his human self and see what habits or creations are there that need to be plucked out, and disposed of; for only by refusing any longer to allow habits of judging, condemning, and criticizing to exist, can he be free. The true activity of the student is only to perfect his own world, and he cannot do it as long as he sees imperfection in the world of another of God's children.

⁊⁊⁊

Oh! the pity mankind have believed so long, and many individuals very sincerely, that they could cure hate, condemnation, and criticism with those same qualities. How futile and tragic has been this false concept. Believe me, Oh Children of the Light! hate never cured hate, and never will. Condemnation and criticism never cured their kind, for as we have often said to you: "That which your attention and vision are held upon, you are qualifying and compelling to come into your world—abide and act there."

Unity and the Science of Man

"But what can I do? I have no great power." Such questions can indicate despair, or a wish to escape responsibility. What the world is, or what a city is, is merely the sum total of the thoughts of each individual. Each of us adds to or subtracts from the good of all of us. The only way the world will ever find peace and harmony is by each individual lifting himself up and recognizing his own spiritual light, and thereby affecting everyone else in the universe. If I speak from a rostrum, a certain number of people will hear my message. If I write down my thoughts and publish them, perhaps more people will be touched. But what I am and what I am thinking at this moment really are affecting every single thing in the world. What a stupendous thought this is: you are important, and you can help to dissolve the problems that divide mankind!

If we find LOVE within ourselves, it is impossible for us not to convey it to others. The more we find within ourselves, the more we will recognize in our brothers. The only way to establish the brotherhood of man on earth is for each of us to begin journeying to the centre of our being—going from the circumference of the flywheel to the centre. This is how we find our spiritual essence; this is the Father within that Jesus talked about. We open ourself to the Spirit of God.

Albert Schweitzer says: "The one thing that truly matters is that we struggle for light to be within us. Each feels the other's struggle, and when a man has light within him it shines out upon others."

This light within us is only made brighter by giving, not taking—by loving, not hating—by serving, not commanding. Material riches are transitory; the only riches worth having are those of the soul (if you do not like the word soul, substitute any word or phrase you like—"that certain something that is the real you").

The world does not lack material things, it lacks awareness

of the light of LOVE. We can define God in one way by saying that God is LOVE, and only by loving will we understand God. The spirit of God is LOVE. Walt Whitman said, "The kelson of creation is LOVE." All illuminated souls have proclaimed this concept of LOVE. All those who founded religions have proclaimed this. But mankind as a whole has never really understood the real meaning of LOVE.

A few men have always been able to apprehend this truth of the brotherhood of man, and they have been responsible for every major advance of mankind. Today more and more people are discovering this truth. They represent the seed of a new type of man—one who understands the meaning of LOVE and unity and brotherhood, who has such reverence for life that he could not possibly do an injustice to his brother.

Science says to us, "LOVE or perish." It is essential that we begin building men and women for the new age of character. Edwin Markham said, "In vain do we build the city if we do not first build the man." Each of us can live to the highest by building himself into a person of character—not just surface honesty, but deep soul integrity.

We dare not allow our governments or institutions to take the responsibility. Each of us must search his soul and find the light of LOVE—and eventually we will realize that each of us is an important radiating centre of this light. Then we can extend ourself in service (indeed, with the awareness of this light within we cannot help but serve).

Jesus gave directions to help us find our way: "Seek first his kingdom," and, "LOVE one another." We must not delegate this to anyone or any organization; the only true growth is through one's own efforts. If each of us begins to live in the light of his own illumination from within, our churches will become places where we can come together to share our experiences of God with one another—not places that separate us into various camps of belief.

"What we believe in is not nearly as important as what we are."

Would you like to have people say to you as you walk down

the street, "There goes a rich man, or a powerful government official,"—or would you rather have them say: "There goes a man of LOVE. Can't you feel it radiating out from him?"

The message is simple: LOVE or perish. Now is the time to make the choice. We begin with ourselves.

The Love Commandments

Most leaders in the spiritual and psychological fields would probably agree that the finest guidelines for human behaviour are to be found in the two "LOVE" commandments:

"You shall LOVE the Lord God with all your heart, and with all your soul, and with all your strength, and with all your mind,"

and

"You shall LOVE your neighbour as yourself."

Why are these commandments so often overlooked and generally ignored? One of the reasons could be that they are presented as rules of conduct or regulations that we should live up to, and there is a natural resistance in us against being told what we should do. I find that a mind-stretching and refreshing way to consider the LOVE commandments is to look at them as prophecy rather than law—as a prescription, rather than as rules of conduct.

These commandments tell us that the point comes in our spiritual growth when we can really begin to exercise the greatest talent, the most tremendous energy in the self-expression equipment of humanity—our ability to LOVE!

Any talent, whether it is of the mind, heart, or muscle is developed through one activity, exercise! Our ability to LOVE is no exception. It grows through exercise . . . exercise . . . exercise!

Often, rather than exercise our ability to LOVE, we exercise our ability to question; we demand to know the answers to ancient queries like these: What is LOVE? Who is the Lord my God? Who is my neighbour? Who am I? Do I have to LOVE those whom I don't like?

Our ability to LOVE is as real as our biceps. If we decide to develop a muscle, we know what to do—not ask questions such as: What is muscle? What is exercise? What is this and what is that? No, if we really want to develop that muscle, we simply start to use it, to exercise it. Many of the questions we have asked will be answered as we exercise!

Your ability to LOVE, then, is your greatest talent, your richest asset. Exercise it with growing confidence, joy, and enthusiasm.

Following are some mind stretchers in words to develop your ability to LOVE:

I accept the LOVE commandments as a prophecy and pre-scription for my own growth and unfoldment. I am ready to exercise my greatest talent, my highest potential—my growing ability to LOVE. I am willing to set aside my questions, knowing that they will be answered as I exercise.

I rejoice and give thanks for my growing ability to LOVE the Lord my God with all my heart, with all my soul, with all my mind, and with all my strength.

I am delighted with my growing ability to LOVE my neighbour as myself.

Even if these exercises seem to be mostly words and vague thoughts right now, I keep exercising, knowing that at least part of my verbal and mental equipment is getting into the act of loving and that the rest of me will follow inevitably.

Unveiled Mysteries

It is very important to realize fully that God's intent for every one of His children is abundance of every good and perfect thing. He created Perfection and endowed His children with exactly the same power. They can create and maintain Perfection also and express God-Dominion over the earth and all that is therein. Mankind was originally created in the Image and Likeness of God. The only reason all do not manifest Dominion is because they do not use their Divine Authority, that with which each individual is endowed and by which he is intended to govern his world. Thus they are not obeying the Law of Love by pouring out peace and blessing to all creation.

✦✦✦

You give little attention, and still less adoration to your "Source"—the Supreme, the Mighty, the Radiant, the Majestic, the Infinite Cause of all that is—the Creator and Sustainer of all worlds. You give no gratitude to the "Great Glorious Presence"—the Lord of Love, for the very Life by which you exist. Oh! Why are you not even grateful for the blessings nature pours out so lavishly, for the abundance that comes to you through this fair land, and from your own wise and unselfish Ruler? You thank each other for favours—the things of the senses and form that are so ephemeral that pass from one to another, and then are no more; but why, oh why! do you forget the *Source* of all Life, all Love, all Intelligence, all Power?

✦✦✦

When the children of earth look away from Love, they are deliberately and consciously choosing the experience of chaos. Whoever seeks to exist without Love cannot survive long anywhere in creation. . . . Whatever lacks Love must return to chaos the unformed, so its substance may be used over again in combination with Love, and thus produce a new and perfect Form. This is the Law of the Universal as well as the individual Life. It is Immutable, Irrevocable, Eternal yet Beneficent, for creation in form exists that God may have something upon which to pour out Love and so express in action.

↗↗↗

Eternal youth is the Flame of God abiding in the body of man—the Father's Gift of Himself to His Creation. Youth and beauty of both mind and body can only be kept *permanently* by those individuals who are strong enough to shut out discord, and whoever does that can and will express Perfection and maintain it. Youth, Beauty, and Perfection are attributes of Love which the God Self is continually pouring forth into Its Creation.

↗↗↗

Watch, so nothing goes out from you except that which is harmonious, and do not allow a destructive word to pass your lips even in jest.

↗↗↗

There is only ONE LAW OF LIFE, and that is LOVE. The Self-Conscious, thinking individual who will not or does not obey that Eternal, Beneficent Decree, cannot, and will not retain the physical body because all that is not LOVE dissolves form and it matters not whether it be thought, word, feeling, or deed —intentional or unintentional—the Law acts regardless. Thoughts, feelings, words, and deeds are each but so much force acting, and eternally move in an orbit of their own. If a man knew that he never ceases creating even for an instant, he would realize, through the "Presence" of God within himself, he could purify his miscreations and thus be free from his own limitations.

↗↗↗

If you will make yourself an Eternal Fountain of Divine Love, pouring it forth into every place your thought goes, you will become such a Magnet for ALL GOOD that you will have to call for help to dispense it. Peace and Calmness of Soul release a Power which compels obedience of the outer mind. This must be *claimed* with authority.

↑↑↑

The great Cosmic Law does not discriminate any more than does the multiplication table, if one makes a mistake in its application, or electricity, when one who is ignorant of the Law governing its use tries to direct its forces without knowledge of the way to control it. The Great Immutable Decrees, which forever keep order in the Infinite Realm of manifested Life are all based upon the One Great Principle of Creation—LOVE. That is the Heart—the Source of ALL and the very HUB upon which existence in form takes place.

Love is Harmony and without it in the beginning of a form, that form could not come into existence at all. LOVE is the cohesive POWER of the Universe, and without it, a Universe could not be.

↑↑↑

Whoever makes himself willingly obedient unto the "Law of Love" has Perfection in his mind and world permanently maintained unto him and him alone does ALL AUTHORITY and MASTERY belong. He *only* has the right to *rule* because he has first learned to obey. . . . Thus mankind through thought and feeling has the power—each individual within himself—to rise to the highest or sink to the lowest. Each one alone determines his own pathway of experience. By conscious control of his attention, as to what he allows his mind to accept, he can walk and talk with God—Face to Face—or looking away from God, become lower than the animals, sinking his human consciousness into oblivion.

Keep a True Lent

Divine Love is the force that dissolves all the opposers of true thought and thus smooths out every obstacle that presents itself. When Love ascends the throne, and takes complete possession of our life, its rule is just and righteous. Even destructive faculties such as resistance, opposition, obstinacy, anger, and jealousy are harmonized through Love. Perfect Love casts out all fear. When Love harmonizes the consciousness, we find that our outer affairs are put in order and that where once there seemed to be opposition and fear cooperation and trust prevail.

✦✦✦

The dissolving power of spiritual Love is the antidote for a dictatorial will, but we must deny all selfish desires out of our Love before we use it in softening the imperious will. Unselfish Love is fearless, because of its forgetfulness of self. They that Love without the adulteration of selfishness or the lust of sense, come into the very presence of God.

✦✦✦

All Love is divine in its origin, but in passing through the prism of man's mind it is apparently broken into many colours. Yet like the ray of white light, it ever remains pure. It is within Man's province to make its manifestation in his life, just as pure as its origin. We learn by experience that Love must be directed by wisdom. If we give up blindly to the impulses suggested by human Love, we shall suffer many downfalls.

✦✦✦

One good definition of Love is that it is the feeling that excites desire for the welfare of its object. If all people would recognize Love as embodying this ideal—recognize that God loves all men to the degree that he has poured out His life, and substance and intelligence equally with us in the universal scheme, they would find in it the solution to every problem of life.

↑↑↑

Many persons wonder why they do not develop divine Love more quickly. Here is the reason: They make a wall of separation between the religious and the secular, between the good and the bad. Divine Love sees no distinction among persons. It is principle and it feels its own perfection everywhere. It feels the same in the heart of the sinner, as it does in the heart of the saint. When we let the Truth of Being into our heart, and pull down all walls of separation, we shall feel the flow of infinite Love that Jesus felt.

↑↑↑

A sense of oneness is a natural product of Love and it is accompanied by a consciousness of security. Through our sense of oneness with the All-Good, the greatest sense of security is realized; therefore all fear is readily and completely cast out. John emphasizes the fact that in order to Love God, we must necessarily Love our fellowmen. A Love that is adulterated in any degree by hatred for anything or anybody is not pure enough to discern the great Love of the Infinite which unifies all men.

↑↑↑

Divine Love is such a transcendent thing that words describing it seem flat and stale. But words used in the right understanding quicken the mind, and we should not despise them. Affirming that we do Love God with all our heart, with all our soul, with all our mind, and with all our might, will cause us to feel a Love we have never felt before. No better treatment for the realization of divine Love can be given than that which Jesus recommended.

↗↗↗

The spirit of obedience is the spirit of Love. Love is the most obedient thing in the universe. It is also the greatest worker, and will accomplish more for our happiness than all other faculties combined. If you want a servant that will work for you night and day, cultivate divine Love. At times there may be obstacles in the mind that interfere with this fellowship of Love. One of them is the thought that we owe our neighbour something besides Love. For some wrong, fancied or otherwise, we think we owe him punishment. The higher power tells us that we owe him Love only, and by sending him the word of Love the law is fulfilled, and the barrier is burned away. We must make friends with everybody and everything in order to have this mighty worker, Love, carry out for us the divine law.

↗↗↗

When we faintly realise the Love of God we begin to Love our fellowmen. There is a fervent Love among Christians that is not to be found among any other group. Love is a divine ordinance, and those who let the Love of God pour itself out in charity do truly cover and forgive a "multitude of sins," not only in themselves but in others; Love pours its balm over every wound, and the substance of its sympathy infuses hope and faith to the discouraged heart.

Divine Love has a balm for every ill.

↗↗↗

Love in Divine Mind is the idea of universal Unity. In expression, it is the power that joins and binds together the universe and everything in it. Love is a harmonizing constructive power. When it is made active in consciousness, it conserves substance, and reconstructs, rebuilds, and restores man and his world.

111

Love is that mighty power, that divine quality of God that is expressing through all mankind, and cannot be suppressed by any outside force.

The word *Love* overcomes hate, resistance, opposition, obstinacy, anger, jealousy, and all other error states where there is mental or physical friction. As divine Love enters into the thought process, every cell of my body is poised and balanced in space, in right mathematical order as to weight and relative distance.

The Search for Personal Freedom

It is not enough, when we are faced with an inharmonious situation, to mouth clichés of absolute Truth: "God is LOVE." "LOVE will solve everything." "LOVE is the greatest thing in the world." Many of us on the spiritual path become metaphysical sloganeers. We delight in the accumulation of affirmations and statements of Truth. However, as Berdyaev says, "Freedom cannot be a form of self-defence: it must lead to creative activity." It is not enough to say, "LOVE will solve the world's problems." LOVE will not solve anything; LOVING will. LOVE is an abstract concept, but LOVING is a creative flow of dynamic energy that harmonizes and dissolves conflicts.

We say, "Faith can take care of any need." Actually, faith without works is nothing, as the wise have always taught. However, when we choose to deal with things in the attitude of faith, and when that faith leads us into works of faith, then there is no limit to what we can do.

Thus it is a matter of using abstract Truth in concrete ways. We often refer to "practical Christianity." But it is only practical when it is practiced. It is so easy to collect and parrot metaphysical propositions and affirmations of Truth; but there is a great need to translate them into dynamic activities set into operation by a conscious act of volition. We must choose to use the truth we know.

All of us have the desire to be free, to be whole, to conquer fear and worry, to live as we would like to live and do what we want to do. This desire is built into our very nature. The trouble is that we have been so busy seeking freedom from certain things that we have not considered alternatives. What do we want freedom to do? We must remember that the truth not only makes us free from pain: it also gives us the freedom to be whole. It not only sets us free from lack: it gives us the freedom to be prosperous and successful.

The urge to be free is misconstrued as simply the desperate

longing to "get out from under," to be free from painful, unbearable conditions. This is why so many run away from a marriage, only to become quickly involved in another equally unbearable relationship. The labour market is crowded with frustrated workers who run from job to job, constantly exercising their prerogative to be free from, but never facing up to themselves so as to make the creative choice to be free to apply their particular talents in the direction of success and fulfillment.

Emerson says, "There is guidance for each of us, and by lowly listening we shall hear the right word." We need to learn to listen in the very depths of ourselves, to "plug in" to the creative potential within us. We cannot really understand the full meaning of freedom, or gain its full benefits, until we begin to respond to the spontaneous activity of our whole personality. Spontaneous is a wonderful word. It comes from the Latin root "sponte," which means "of one's free will." Spontaneous activity is the free activity of the self.

↑↑↑

If I lift my hand spontaneously, without concern about what another person may think, I am doing what I want to do. If I have the urge to laugh or cry or sing or whistle—and do so spontaneously—then I am free. But if I am with a friend who is crying, and I have the urge to put my arms around him and express the warmth of my sincere LOVE—and don't do it—I am inhibited. I am in bondage. If I shun involvement with people even though I hunger for LOVE and affection and friendship, I am not free. And my knowledge of Truth is a mere pastime if it does not set me free to do so and be that which I am impelled to do by my "high yearning."

Catherine Lawes, the wife of the former warden of Sing Sing, used to go into the yard of the prison almost every day. When the men played games, her children would play with them. She would sit with other prisoners and watch. People told her that this was not good, not safe. She would say, "But these men are my friends." She died suddenly and word spread through the prison. The men gathered as close to the gate as possible, responding to the great LOVE they had felt from this wonderful woman. The gatekeeper, watching the eagerness and sincere feeling of the prisoners, spontaneously, and without any order flung open the gate. All day long the men filed to the house outside the walls where the body of Catherine Lawes lay. There were no walls around them, yet not one prisoner broke the trust that had been placed in him. They all reported back to the prison.

The prisoners had actually been given a measure of freedom through the LOVE of Catherine Lawes. This freedom was more important to them than the fact that they were locked behind walls of stone and steel. This inner spirit of freedom was more important even than the experience of freedom when they were released to visit the home where she had passed away. Through the creative act of LOVING, they were given a kind of freedom that transcended cells and bars and keepers.

Perhaps this is an insight into what true freedom really is. Perhaps something like the creative act of LOVE may be the most important means of achieving personal freedom, and giving that freedom to the world. Freedom, as most of us have sought it, has been the attempt to get freedom from things: from oppression, from people, from problems, from pain, from insecurity. We need to begin to think of it in a more creative sense: the freedom to be, to become something, to be big enough to deal with the experience of life. Not just freedom to erase difficulties, and eliminate persons (as we may be subconsciously desiring), but rather freedom to release our own spiritual capacities.

When we understand this, we will begin to let go—not only of our problems, but also of our rigid metaphysical concepts about them—and then walk on and begin each day anew in our quest for understanding. We will make a commitment to translate abstract truths into creative acts.

Teilhard de Chardin says: "Someday, after mastering the winds, the waves, the tides, and gravity, we shall harness the energies of LOVE, and then for the second time in the history of the world, man will discover fire."

People Are Like Poems

People are like great works of art. Fall in LOVE with them and you may see clear through to reality.

Have you ever had a great work of art—a poem or a piece of music or a painting—open its soul and reveal itself to you?

Great works of art have a kind of hidden luminosity about them. A poem, for instance, is just some lines, on a page in a book. But once in a while, if you fall in LOVE with it, a poem reveals itself to you. The lines glow, and suddenly you see through the words into life. You see truth as if it were a clear shining light.

People are like that. They, too, glow with a kind of hidden luminosity when you get past the obvious.

Our Finest Hour

There is so much controversy in the world today as intellect meets intellect in theory and in practice. Minds try to solve the problems of this modern day from the outer, without reaching the basic cause and premise within. Psychologist disagrees with psychologist, religionist with religionist, politician with politician, physician with physician, and friend with friend. Sometimes we are thrown into a complete fog as we listen and read the many conflicting opinions in this tired world.

Where do we turn? What do we do? Many of us have had beliefs that have sustained us in years past that no longer are adequate. We shake inside at the thought of abandoning them, yet we shake as we see them fail again and again in the world about us. The quandary is, do we stay with the outmoded ideas of our forefathers or leave them for a trackless path, an unscaled way—to where or to what?

It is very difficult to forsake the old—but it has already forsaken us and leaves us no alternative but to move into the unknown. All great religious leaders of the world are those who have stood against the culture that was acceptable in their time. All permanent progress has been made by rebellion against and conflict with things as they are. Socrates, Moses, Jesus, and Luther were forced to stand alone against the great minds and ideas of their day.

To be a leader in your own soul and mind and body, you must think for yourself and not be swayed by every breeze of opinion. If you are to live a balanced true life, you must be in charge of your own life.

Prayer of Thanksgiving: I Am Receptive

I have opened my mind and heart to these teachings and have learned that the true nature of the Spirit within me and within all God's creation is LOVE. I have learned that only when this LOVE is expressed by all, fully and freely, will the kingdom of heaven be established right here on earth. I have learned that only I can hinder the expression of God's LOVE through me by being unresponsive to the efforts of the Spirit to use me as an instrument. I have learned that Love attracts Love, and so in the measure that I let God's LOVE flow through me it will also flow through those whose lives touch mine.

I accept the challenge now to put what I have learned into practice. I would let no thought that does not pass the test of LOVE take root in my mind. I would let no word that is not borne on the cushion of LOVE escape my lips. I would let no act that is not loving in intent demean my relationships. I see nothing in me that would block the expression of God's LOVE.

Each day I give thanks that a greater measure of the Spirit of LOVE within me unfolds. Each day with joy and delight I see more evidence of the activity of LOVE in those around me, and it is beautiful. Looking through eyes of LOVE I see myself as part of the unity of all things. My life takes on new meaning and purpose as I bring forth through LOVE the highest that is in all persons, the best that is in all situations. Truly I have learned that life is for loving, and I help to make the world a better place as I follow the teaching of the Master, "If ye know these things, blessed are ye if ye do them."